Path-Oriented Program Analysis

This book presents a unique method for decomposing a computer program along its execution paths, for simplifying the subprograms so produced, and for recomposing a program from its subprograms. This method enables us to divide and conquer the complexity involved in understanding the computation performed by a program by decomposing it into a set of subprograms and then simplifying them to the furthest extent possible. The resulting simplified subprograms are generally more understandable than the original program as a whole. The method may also be used to simplify a piece of source code by following the path-oriented method of decomposition, simplification, and recomposition. The analysis may be carried out in such a way that the derivation of the analysis result constitutes a correctness proof. The method can be applied to any source code (or portion thereof) that prescribes the computation to be performed in terms of assignment statements, conditional statements, and loop constructs, regardless of the language or paradigm used.

J. C. Huang received a Ph.D. in electrical engineering from the University of Pennsylvania in 1969. He is a Professor Emeritus in the Department of Computer Science at the University of Houston, where he served as chair from 1992 to 1996.

His practical experience in computer software includes serving as the chief architect of a software validation and verification system developed for the U.S. Army's Ballistic Missile Defense Command, and as a senior consultant to the U.S. Naval Underwater Systems Center on submarine software problems.

Path-Oriented Program Analysis

J. C. Huang
University of Houston, Houston, Texas

CAMBRIDGE
UNIVERSITY PRESS

CAMBRIDGE UNIVERSITY PRESS
Cambridge, New York, Melbourne, Madrid, Cape Town, Singapore, São Paulo, Delhi

Cambridge University Press
32 Avenue of the Americas, New York, NY 10013-2473, USA

www.cambridge.org
Information on this title: www.cambridge.org/9780521882866

First published 2008

Printed in the United States of America

A catalog record for this publication is available from the British Library.

Library of Congress Cataloging in Publication Data

Huang, J. C., 1935–
Path-oriented program analysis / J. C. Huang
    p.   cm.
Includes bibliographical references and index.
ISBN-978-0-521-88286-6 (hardback)
1. Computer software – Development.   2. Computer software –
Development – Computer programs.   I. Title.
QA76.76.D47H83   2008
005.1 – dc22   2007026404

ISBN   978-0-521-88286-6 hardback

To my wife

Contents

Contents

Preface

Many years ago, I was given the responsibility of leading a large software project. The aspect of the project that worried me the most was the correctness of the programs produced. Whenever a part of the product became suspect, I could not put my mind to rest until the product was tested successfully with a well-chosen set of test cases and until I was able to understand the source code in question clearly and completely. It was not always easy to understand. That was when I started to search for ways to facilitate program understanding.

A program can be difficult to understand for many reasons. The difficulty may stem, for example, from the reader's unfamiliarity with the application area, from the obscurity of the algorithm implemented, or from the complex logic used in organizing the source code. Given the different reasons that difficulty may arise, a single comprehensive solution to this problem may never be found.

I realized, however, that the creator of a program must always decompose the task to be performed by the program to the extent that it can be prescribed in terms of the programming language used. If the

Preface

reader could see exactly how the task was decomposed, the difficulty of understanding the code would be eased because the reader could separately process each subprogram, which would be smaller in size and complexity than the program as a whole.

The problem is that the decomposition scheme deployed in any program may not be immediately obvious from the program text. This is so because programmers use code sharing to make source code compact and avoid unnecessary repetition. Code sharing, together with certain syntactic constraints imposed by programming languages, tends to obscure the decomposition scheme embodied in any program. Some analysis is required to recover this information.

Mathematically speaking, there are three basic ways to decompose a function. The first way is to divide the computation to be performed into a sequence of smaller steps. The second way is to compute a function with many arguments in terms of functions of fewer arguments. The third way is to partition the input domain into a number of subdomains and prescribe the computation to be performed for each subdomain separately. Methods already exist to recover and exploit information relevant to the first two decomposition schemes: They are known as the techniques of symbolic execution and program slicing, respectively. This book presents an analysis method that allows us to extract, analyze, and exploit information relevant to the third decomposition scheme.

Do not be intimidated by the formalisms found in the text. The theorems and corollaries are simply rules designed to manipulate programs. To be precise and concise, formulas in first-order predicate calculus are used to describe the rules. Only elementary knowledge of symbolic logic is needed to interpret those rules.

Typically, the method described in this book is to be used as follows. The program in question is test-executed with an input. If the program produces an incorrect result, it is a definite indication that the program is faulty, and appropriate action must be taken to locate and correct the fault. On the other hand, if the program produces a correct result, one can conclude with certainty only that the program is correct for that particular input. One can broaden the significance of the test result, however, by finding the execution path traversed during the test-execution and then applying the analysis method presented in this book to determine

(1) the conditions under which the same path will be traversed, and (2) the exact nature of the computation performed during execution. This information about execution paths in the program can then be integrated to obtain a better understanding of the program as a whole. This method is illustrated in Appendix A with example programs in C++.

This book contains enough information for the reader to apply the method manually. Manual application of this method, however, is inevitably tedious and error prone. To use the method in a production environment, the method must be mechanized. Software tool designers will find the formal basis presented in this work useful in creating a detailed design.

Being able to understand programs written by others is of practical importance. It is a skill that is fundamental to anyone who reuses software or who is responsible for software quality assurance and beneficial to anyone who designs programs, because it allows designers to learn from others. It is a skill that is not easy to acquire. I am not aware of any academic institution that offers a course on the subject. Typically, students learn to understand programs by studying small examples found in programming textbooks, and they may never be challenged, while in school, to understand a real-world program. Indeed, I have often heard it said – and not only by students – that if a program is difficult to understand, it must be badly written and thus should be rewritten or discarded. Program analysis is normally covered in a course on compiler construction. The problem is that what is needed to make a compiler compile is not necessarily the same as what is needed to make a programmer understand. We need methods to facilitate program understanding. I hope that publication of this book will motivate further study on the subject.

I would like to take this opportunity to thank William E. Howden for his inspiration; Raymond T. Yeh for giving me many professional opportunities that allowed this method to develop from conception, through various stages of experimentation, and finally to the present state of maturity; and John L. Bear and Marc Garbey for giving me the time needed to complete the writing of this book. I would also like to thank Heather Bergman for seeking me out and encouraging me to publish this work and Pooja Jain for her able editorial assistance in getting the book produced. Finally, my heartfelt thanks go to my daughter, Joyce, for her

Preface

active and affectionate interest in my writing, and for her invaluable help in the use of the English language, and to my wife, Shihwen, for her support, and for allowing me to neglect her while getting this work done.

J. C. Huang
Houston

1

Introduction

Program analysis is a problem area concerned with methodical extraction of information from programs. It has attracted a great deal of attention from computer scientists since the inception of computer science as an academic discipline. Earlier research efforts were mostly motivated by problems encountered in compiler construction (Aho and Ullman, 1973). Subsequently, the problem area was expanded to include those that arise from development of computer-aided software engineering tools, such as the question of how to detect certain programming errors through static analysis (Fosdick and Osterweil, 1976).

By the mid-1980s, the scope of research in program analysis had greatly expanded to include, among others, investigation of problems in data-flow equations, type inference, and closure analysis. Each of these problem areas was regarded as a separate research domain with its own terminology, problems, and solutions.

Gradually, efforts to extend the methods started to emerge and to produce interesting results. It is now understood that those seemingly disparate problems are related, and we can gain much by studying them in a unified conceptual framework. As the result, there has been a dramatic shift in the research directions in recent years. A great deal of research effort has been directed to investigate the possibilities of extending and combining existent results [see, e.g., Aiken (1999); Amtoft et al. (1999); Cousot and Cousot (1977); Flanagan and Qadeer (2003); and Jones and Nielson (1995)].

In the prevailing terminology, we can say that there are four major approaches to program analysis, viz., data-flow analysis, constraint-based analysis, abstract interpretation, and type-and-effect system (Nielson et al., 2005).

The definition of data-flow analysis appears to have been broadened considerably. In the classical sense, data-flow analysis is a process of collecting data-flow information about a program. Examples of data-flow information include facts about where a variable is assigned a value, where that value is used, and whether or not that value will be used again downstream. Compilers use such information to perform transformations like constant folding and dead-code elimination (Aho et al., 1986). In the recent publications one can now find updated definitions of data-flow analysis, such as "data-flow analysis computes its solutions over the paths in a control-flow graph" (Ammons and Larus, 1998) and the like.

Constraint-based analysis consists of two parts: constraint generation and constraint resolution. Constraint generation produces constraints from the program text. The constraints give a declarative specification of the desired information about the program. Constraint resolution then computes this desired information (Aiken, 1999).

Abstract interpretation is a theory of sound approximation of the semantics of computer programs. As aptly explained in the lecture note of Patrick Cousot at MIT, the concrete mathematical semantics of a program is an infinite mathematical object that is not computable. All nontrivial questions on concrete program semantics are undecidable.

A type system defines how a programming language classifies values and expressions into types, how it can manipulate those types, and how they interact. It can be used to detect certain kinds of errors during program development. A type-and-effect system builds on, and extends, the notion of types by incorporating behaviors that are able to track information flow in the presence of procedures, channels based on communication, and the dynamic creation of network topologies (Amtoft et al., 1999).

Introduction

This book presents a path-oriented method for program analysis. The property to be determined in this case is the computation performed by the program and prescribed in terms of assignment statements, conditional statements, and loop constructs. The method is path oriented[1] in that the desired information is to be extracted from the execution paths of the program. We explicate the computation performed by the program by representing each execution path as a subprogram, and then using the rules developed in this work to simplify the subprogram or to rewrite it into a different form.

Because the execution paths are to be extracted by the insertion of constraints into the program to be analyzed, this book may appear to be yet another piece of work in constraint-based analysis in light of the current research directions just outlined. But that is purely coincidental. The intent of this book is simply to present an analysis method that the reader may find it useful in some way. No attempt has been made to connect it to, or fit it into, the grand scheme of current theoretical research in program analysis.

The need for a method like this may arise when a software engineer attempts to determine if a program will do what it is intended to do. A practical way to accomplish this is to test-execute the program for a properly chosen set of test cases (inputs). If the test fails, i.e., if the program produces at least one incorrect result, we know for sure that the program is in error. On the other hand, if all test results produced are correct, we can conclude only that the program works correctly for the test cases used. The strength of this conclusion may prove to be inadequate in some applications. The question then is, what can we do to reinforce our confidence in the program? One possible answer is to read the source code. Other than an elegant formal proof of correctness, probably nothing else is more reassuring than the fact that the source code is clearly understood and test-executes correctly.

It is a fact of life that most of a real-world program is not that difficult to read. But occasionally even a competent software engineer will find

---

[1] This is not to be confused with the term "path sensitive." In some computer science literature (see, e.g., WIKIPEDIA in references), a program analysis method is characterized as being path sensitive if the results produced are valid only on feasible execution paths. In that sense, the present method is not path sensitive, as will become obvious later.

Path-Oriented Program Analysis

a segment of code that defies his or her effort to comprehend. That is when the present method may be called on to facilitate the process.

A piece of source code can be difficult to understand for many different reasons, one of which is the reader's inability to see clearly how the function was decomposed when the code was written to implement it. The present method is designed to help the reader to recover that piece of information.

To understand the basic ideas involved, it is useful to think of a program as an artifact that embodies a mathematical function. As such, it can be decomposed in three different ways.

The first is to decompose f into subfunctions, say, f_1 and f_2, such that $f(x) = f_1(f_2(x))$. In a program, f, f_1, and f_2 are often implemented as assignment statements. The computation it prescribes can be explicated by use of the technique of symbolic execution (King, 1976; Khurshid et al., 2003).

The second is to decompose f into subfunctions, say, f_3, f_4, and f_5, such that

$$f(x, y, z) = f_3(f_4(x, y), f_5(y, z)).$$

In a real program, the code segments that implement f_4 and f_5 can be identified by using the technique of program slicing (Weiser, 1984).

The third way of decomposition is to decompose f into a set of n subfunctions such that

$$f = \{f_1, f_2, \ldots, f_n\},$$
$$f : X \rightarrow Y,$$
$$X = X_1 \cup X_2 \cup \ldots \cup X_n,$$
$$f_i : X_i \rightarrow Y \text{ for all } 1 \leq i \leq n.$$

An execution path in the program embodies one of the subfunctions. The present method is designed to identify, manipulate, and exploit code segments that embody such subfunctions.

Examples are now used to show the reader some of the tasks that can be performed with the present method.

Two comments about the examples used here and throughout this book first.

Programs in C++ are used as examples because C++ is currently one of the most, if not the most, commonly used programming languages at present.

Furthermore, some example programs have been chosen that are contrived and unnecessarily difficult to understand. The reason to keep example programs small is to save space, and the reason to make them difficult to understand is so that the advantages of using the present method can be decisively demonstrated.

Consider the C++ program listed below.

Program 1.1

```
#include <iostream>
#include <string>
using namespace std
int atoi(string& s)
{
    int i, n, sign;
    i = 0;
    while (isspace(s[i]))
        i = i + 1;
    if (s[i] == '-')
        sign = -1;
    else
        sign = 1;
    if (s[i] == '+' || s[i] == '-')
        i = i + 1;
    n = 0;
    while (isdigit(s[i])) {
        n = 10 * n + (s[i] -- '0');
        i = i + 1;
    }
    return sign * n;
}
```

This is a C++ version of a standard library function that accepts a string of digits as input and returns the integer value represented by that string.

Path-Oriented Program Analysis

Now suppose we test-execute this program with input string, say, "7," and the program returns 7 as the value of function atoi. This test result is obviously correct. From this test result, however, we can conclude only that this piece of source code works correctly for this particular input string. As mentioned before, we can bolster our confidence in the correctness of this program by finding the execution path traversed during the test-execution and the answers to the following questions: (1) What is the condition under which this execution path will be traversed? and (2) what computation is performed in the process?

The execution path can be precisely and concisely described by the symbolic trace subsequently listed. The symbolic trace of an execution path is defined to be the linear listing of the statements and true predicates encountered on the path (Howden and Eichorst, 1977).

Trace 1.2

```
i = 0;
/\!(isspace(s[i]));
/\!(s[i] == '-');
sign = 1;
/\!(s[i] == '+' || s[i] == '-');
n = 0;
/\ (isdigit(s[i]));
n = 10 * n + (s[i] - '0');
i = i + 1;
/\!(isdigit(s[i]));
return sign * n;
```

Note that every true path-predicate in the preceding trace is prefixed with a digraph "/\" and terminated with a semicolon.

In comparison with the whole program (Program 1.1), the symbolic trace is simpler in logical structure and smaller in size because all statements irrelevant to this execution are excluded. This symbolic trace contains answers to the two questions previously posed, but the answers are not immediately obvious.

It turns out that we can obtain the desired answers by treating the true predicates on the path as state constraints (see Chapter 2) and by using the rules developed in the following chapters to rewrite the trace into the form that directly reveal the answers.

In particular, we develop a set of rules that can be used to move a constraint up or down the control flow without changing the semantics of the program (see Chapter 3). By repeatedly applying this set of rules to the subprogram, we can obtain an equivalent subprogram with all constraints on the top and all assignment statements at the bottom.

If we apply this step to Trace 1.2, it becomes the following program.

Program 1.3

```
int atoi(string& s)
{
    int i, n, sign;
    /\!(isspace(s[0])) &&!(s[0] == '-');
    /\!(s[0] == '+' || s[0] == '-');
    /\ (isdigit(s[0]));
    /\!(isdigit(s[0+1]));
    i = 0;
    sign = 1;
    n = 0;
    n = 10 * n + (s[i] -- '0');
    i = i + 1;
    return sign * n;
}
```

Note that when constraints are placed immediately next to one another, their relationship becomes that of a logical conjunction. This conjunction of constraints on the upper half of the subprogram often can be greatly simplified because most constraints in the same program are not entirely independent of one another. The most common relationship among constraints is that one is implied by the other. This afford the possibility of simplification because, if A *implies* B, "A *and* B" is reduced to B.

Also note that the long sequence of assignment statements at the bottom of the subprogram can also be simplified by use of the technique of symbolic execution (King, 1975; Khurshid et al., 2003) and the rules developed in this book (Huang, 1990).

Path-Oriented Program Analysis

Program 1.3 can thus be simplified to Program 1.4.[2]

Program 1.4

```
/\ (isdigit(s[0])) && !(isdigit(s[1]));
return s[0] - '0';
```

Program 1.4 says that the computation performed by Program 1.1 can be reduced to a single statement `return s[0] - '0'` if its definition is constrained by the predicate `(isdigit(s[0])) && !(isdigit(s[1]))`. In words, this simplified subprogram says that this subprogram is defined for all input strings consisting of a single digit, and it computes the difference between the ASCII representation of the input digit and that of digit `'0'`.

In a quality-related software process, such as testing, understanding, walkthrough, and constructing correctness proof, it is essential that we be able to describe an execution path precisely and concisely, to determine the condition under which it will be traversed, and to determine the computation it performs while the path is being traversed. As just illustrated, we can use the present method to accomplish this effectively.

It is important to understand clearly that Program 1.4 is not equivalent to the statement

```
if ((isdigit(s[0])) && !(isdigit(s[1])))
return s[0] - '0';
```

Although this conditional statement will do exactly the same as Program 1.4 if the condition `(isdigit(s[0]))&& !(isdigit(s[1]))` is satisfied, it will act differently when the condition is not satisfied: This conditional statement would do nothing (i.e., will maintain *status quo*) whereas Program 1.4 would become undefined, i.e., it would give no information whatsoever!

In abstract, if f is the function implemented by Program 1.1, f is decomposed by the programmer into many subfunctions, each of which is implemented by an execution path in the program. The path described by Trace 1.2 implements one of those. The present method allows us to treat each trace as a subprogram and to transform it to explicate the properties of that subprogram.

---

[2] Details are given in Appendix A.

Two possible relationships among programs are now introduced. Given two programs S_1 and S_2, we say "S_1 is (logically) equivalent to S_2" and write $S_1 \Leftrightarrow S_2$ if and only if S_1 and S_2 have the same input domain and compute the same function. We say "S_2 is a subprogram of S_1" and write $S_1 \Rightarrow S_2$ if and only if the input domain of S_2 is a subset of that of S_1, and, within the input domain of S_2, S_1 and S_2 compute the same function. The formal definitions are given in Chapter 2.

Evidently, Program 1.1 $\Rightarrow$ Program 1.4.

Different constraints can be inserted into Program 1.1 in different ways to create different subprograms. For instance, consider the execution path subsequently listed. It is similar to Trace 1.2 except that the last loop construct in Program 1.1 is iterated one more time.

Program 1.5

```
i = 0;
/\ ! (isspace(s[i]));
/\ ! (s[i] == '-');
sign = 1;
/\ ! (s[i] == '+' || s[i] == '-');
n = 0;
/\ (isdigit(s[i]));
n = 10 * n + (s[i] - '0');
i = i + 1;
/\ (isdigit(s[i]));
n = 10 * n + (s[i] - '0');
i = i + 1;
/\ ! (isdigit(s[i]));
return sign * n;
```

This trace, when treated as a subprogram of Program 1.1, can be similarly simplified to Program 1.6.

Program 1.6

```
/\ (isdigit(s[0])) && (isdigit(s[1]))
    && !(isdigit(s[2]));
return 10 * (s[0] - '0') + (s[1] - '0');
```

Path-Oriented Program Analysis

The first line says that this path will be traversed if the input is a string of two, and only two, digits. The function will return an integer value equal to that of the first digit times 10, plus that of the second digit. Again, that is precisely what `atoi` is designed to do.

State constraints can be used to decompose a program pathwise into subprograms, each of which is smaller and less capable than the original. A *program set* is a construct (as defined in Chapter 4) designed to "glue" two or more programs together to form a new program that is more complex and capable than each of its constituent components.

In abstract, we use ordinary set notation to denote a program set. Thus if we have two programs P_1 and P_2, we can form a program set $\{P_1, P_2\}$, the formal semantics of which are given in Chapter 4. For now it suffices to say that, if program $P = \{P_1, P_2\}$, P is not only defined in the subdomain in which P_1 is defined, it is also defined in the subdomain in which P_2 is defined as well. Furthermore, it has the capability of P_1 as well as that of P_2.

Because the curly braces "{", "}", and comma "," used in ordinary set notation have special meanings in many programming languages, the trigraphs "{{{", "}}}" and ",,," are used instead to prevent possible confusion when those symbols are used in a real program.

Thus a singleton program set consisting of Program 1.4 as its element is written as

```
{{{
    /\ (isdigit(s[0])) &&!(isdigit(s[1])));
    return s[0] - '0';
}}}
```

We can add Program 1.6 into this program set to form a new one:

```
{{{
    /\ (isdigit(s[0])) &&!(isdigit(s[1])));
    return s[0] - '0';
,,,
    /\ (isdigit(s[0])) && (isdigit(s[1]))
        &&!(isdigit(s[2])));
    return 10 * (s[0] - '0') + (s[1] - '0');
}}}
```

This new program set is now defined for all inputs consisting of a single digit; it is also defined for all strings consisting of two digits as well.

In view of Programs 1.4 and 1.6, we can clearly see that the function implemented by Program 1.1 is decomposed in the form mentioned previously:

$f = \{f_1, f_2, \ldots, f_n\}$,
$f : X \rightarrow Y$,
$X = X_1 \cup X_2 \cup \ldots \cup X_n$,
$f_i : X_i \rightarrow Y$ for all $1 \leq i \leq n$,

where $X = \{x \mid x$ is a string of digits$\}$,
$\quad\quad\quad Y = \{y \mid y$ is an integer$\}$,
$\quad\quad\quad X_i = \{x \mid x \in X$ and $length(x) = i\}$,
for any $d_i \ldots d_3 d_2 d_1 \in X_i$, $f_i(d_i \ldots d_3 d_2 d_1) = d_i \times 10^{i-1} + \cdots + d_3 \times 10^2 + d_2 \times 10^1 + d_1 \times 10^0$, and n = the maximum length of string that can be accepted by function atoi.

This analysis result should be helpful in understanding how function atoi converts a string of digits into the decimal integer represented by that string. And if the analysis was performed to support the result of a successful test, it should bolster our confidence in the correctness of this program substantially.

The reader might have noticed that, up to this point, only procedure-oriented (vs. object-oriented) programs have been chosen as examples. The choices were made to simplify explanation of the principles involved but in no way to imply that the applicability of the present analysis method is confined to procedure-oriented programs. Actually, the method can be applied to object-oriented programs as well. It follows from the fact that both traditional and object-oriented programs perform computation in a similar manner. The fundamental difference is in the way a program is organized, i.e., in the way an execution path is divided up and incorporated in different parts of the program. The sequence of steps to be taken to compute a function is the same. The algorithm used, not the way the program is organized, determines the sequence.

Example A.4 in Appendix is constructed to demonstrate this point. C++ programmers should also be able to see the applicability in Example

Path-Oriented Program Analysis

A.3 as well. Although Program A.3 is written as a function of a procedure-oriented program, the same code can be used *mutatis mutandis* as a member function of a class in an object-oriented program. The present method can be applied to analyze that piece of code equally well, either as a "function" or as a "method" in the program.

It should be reiterated here that the present method is designed to explicate the computation prescribed in terms of assignment statements, conditional statements, and loop constructs. To apply the method, the user must be able to find relevant execution paths in the code to be analyzed, either manually or through the use of a software tool. This ability is always tacitly assumed. The task, however, may be made more complex by multithreading, call-backs, virtual method calls, reflection, and other features of a modern distributed object-oriented software system, discussion of which is beyond the scope of this work.

With the problems and possible solutions that motivated the development of the present analysis method now explained, it is now ready to be presented fully in the following chapters.

To make it possible to work with execution paths, two new programming constructs called *state constraint* and *program set* were introduced. These are formally defined and discussed in detail in Chapters 2 and 4, respectively.

State constraints are designed to be inserted into a program to create subprograms. Chapter 3 shows how to insert constraints in such a way that it will yield subprograms with simple logical structures. In particular, we can use appropriate constraints to produce subprograms that represent execution paths in the program. It is observed that such subprograms can be further simplified if we can segregate the constraints from the program statements. For that purpose, a set of rules that allow constraints to be moved upstream is presented. By moving all constraints upstream, we will be left with a subprogram with all constraints on the top, and statements on the bottom. Such a subprogram tends to be more amendable to further simplification.

Chapter 4 introduces a new programming construct called a program set that can be used to "glue" subprograms together to form a new, larger, and more capable program. With this mechanism, we can now formulate a general strategy for program simplification: Given a program, decompose it pathwise into a set of subprograms; use the rules developed in the present method to simplify each subprogram and then recompose the simplified subprograms into a whole. The result is a simpler program equivalent to the original.

To help envision how a program is decomposed pathwise or how a set of subprograms is glued together, Chapter 5 presents a way to represent a piece of source code as a program graph. A program graph is a directed graph in which every edge is associated with a pair $(/\backslash C, S)$, where $/\backslash C$ is a constraint and S is a sequence of statements. Because a path structure of a directed graph can be described by a regular expression over the edge symbols, a program can thus be described by a regular expression over a set of pairs of the form $(/\backslash C, S)$. This representation scheme allows us to describe path structures in a precise and concise manner.

Next, it is observed that, after a program statement is executed, it causes a condition to become true. For example, after execution of the assignment statement $X = 10$, condition $X == 10$ becomes true. Thus, if we place the constraint $/\backslash X = 10$ immediately after the statement $X = 10$, it would not change the semantics of the program. Such a constraint is said to be tautological. In Chapter 6 it is shown that tautological constraints can be inserted into a program to facilitate program analysis and discarded after the analysis is completed. It can also be used to construct a program correctness proof. In fact, the present method can be used to construct a correctness proof in a top-down manner similar to the inductive assertion method [see, e.g., Anderson (1979)] or in a bottom-up manner similar to Dijkstra's predicate transformation method [see, e.g., Yeh (1977)].

Previously it was mentioned that we can simplify a program by decomposing it into a set of subprograms, simplifying each subprogram, and then recomposing the simplified subprograms into a whole. Examples are used to show how this can be done in Chapter 7. The problem is that a loop construct may be decomposed into a prohibitively large number of subprograms. Can we recompose a loop construct from a finite and manageably small number of trace subprograms? The answer is affirmative, and the process is illustrated in Chapter 7.

A loop construct in the program may create another problem, i.e., it may create a set of trace subprograms, each of which is defined for only one element in the input domain. In that case, we can gain little by generating the trace subprogram and simplifying it to the extent possible because the result will show how the computation is performed for that particular input only. The same result can be obtained with less effort through a test-execution. Chapter 8 shows how the present method can be used to solve a problem of this sort. It also shows how the graphic representation of programs introduced in Chapter 5 can be utilized to construct a rigorous proof of the equivalence of certain loop constructs. The simplicity of the proof is probably not achievable through other means.

The usefulness of the present method can be significantly enhanced by building software tools to instrument the program automatically for trace-subprogram generation and to aid application of the rules to manipulate the subprograms. Chapter 9 discusses how to instrument a C++ program for automatic generation of trace subprograms.

Finally, several examples are included in Appendix A to show how the rules are applied, and how the desired results can be derived from a program in detail. Appendix B contains some background materials in logic, mathematics, and graph theory that are needed to understand this work fully.

2

State Constraints

Consider[1] a restrictive clause of this form:

The program state at this point must satisfy predicate C, or else the program becomes undefined.

By program state here we mean the aggregate of values assumed by all variables involved. Because this clause constrains the states assumable by the program, it is called a *state constraint*, or a *constraint* for short, and is denoted by $/\backslash C$.

State constraints are designed to be inserted into a program to create another program. For instance, given a program of the form of Program 2.1, a new program can be created, as shown in Program 2.2.

---

[1] Chapters 2–5 include materials from a previous publication © 1990 IEEE. Reprinted with permission from Huang, J.C., "State constraints and pathwise decomposition of programs," *IEEE Transactions on Software Engineering* **16**, 880–896 (1990).

Path-Oriented Program Analysis

Program 2.1

$S_1; S_2.$

Program 2.2

$S_1; /\!\backslash\ C; S_2.$

Program 2.2 is said to be created from Program 2.1 by constraining the program states to C prior to execution of S_2. Intuitively, Program 2.2 is a subprogram of Program 2.1 because its definition is that of Program 2.1 restricted to C. Within that restriction, Program 2.2 performs the same computation as Program 2.1.

A state constraint is a semantic modifier. The meaning of a program modified by a state constraint can be formally defined in terms of Dijkstra's (1976) weakest precondition[2] as follows. Let S be a programming construct and C be a predicate, then for any postcondition R,

Axiom 2.3

$wp(/\!\backslash\ C;S, R) \equiv C \land wp(S, R).$

Of course a constraint can also be inserted after a program. For economy of expression, we say we *preconstrain* program S with constraint C if we write $/\!\backslash\ C;S$, and *postconstrain* program S with constraint C if we write $S;/\!\backslash\ C$.

A comparison of similar entities subsequently listed should help to sharpen the idea just introduced:

> *State constraint*: The purpose is to restrict the domain of definition. The processor evaluates its truth-value. The program becomes undefined if it is evaluated to false.

---

[2] The weakest precondition of program S with respect to postcondition Q, commonly denoted by wp(S, Q), is defined as the weakest condition for the initial state of S such that activation of S will certainly result in a properly terminating happening, leaving S in a final state satisfying Q (Dijkstra, 1975).

Branch or loop predicate: The purpose is to alter the flow of control. The processor evaluates its truth-value. If it is false, an alternative path is taken.

Constraint in the constraint programming languages (Leller, 1988): The purpose is to define a relation that must be maintained throughout the program. The processor finds appropriate values of variables to satisfy the constraint. If it is found unsatisfiable, a programming error occurs.

Constraint in ADA (Gehani, 1983): It is used to specify further restrictions on the values that may be held by the variables, besides the restriction that the values must belong to the type specified by the type mark. The processor evaluates its truth-value. If it is false, an exception is raised, but the definition of the program remains intact.

Constraint used in artificial intelligence: The purpose is to limit the values assumable by variables that occur in a description (Charniak and McDermott, 1985). The processor evaluates its truth-value. A false constraint signifies the inapplicability of the description.

Assertion inserted in proving program correctness (Anderson, 1979) *or dynamic assertion checking* (Stucki, 1973): It is used to check the states assumed by the program and does not modify the program in any way. The processor evaluates its truth-value. The program is in error if it is evaluated to false.

Constraint in constraint-based program analysis (Aiken, 1999): As explained briefly in Chapter 1, we can perform analysis on a program by inserting constraints on strategic points in the program and solving the constraints to produce the desired results. The idea is very similar except that in general there is no need to solve the constraints in the present method. We obtain the desired results by using the constraints to rewrite or to simplify the program.

Definition 2.4

Program S_1 is said to be *equivalent to* S_2 if $wp(S_1, R) \equiv wp(S_2, R)$ for any postcondition R. This relation is denoted by $S_1 \Leftrightarrow S_2$.

It is easy to show that the "equivalent" relation ($\Leftrightarrow$) just defined is (1) *reflexive*, i.e., $S \Leftrightarrow S$, (2) *symmetric*, i.e., if $S_1 \Leftrightarrow S_2$ then $S_2 \Leftrightarrow S_1$, and

(3) *transitive*, i.e., if $S_1 \Leftrightarrow S_2$ and $S_2 \Leftrightarrow S_3$ then $S_1 \Leftrightarrow S_3$. That is to say, "$\Leftrightarrow$" is an equivalence relation in the mathematical sense.

Definition 2.5

Program S_2 is said to be a *subprogram* of program S_1 if $wp(S_2, R) \supset wp(S_1, R)$ for any postcondition R. This relation is denoted by $S_1 \Rightarrow S_2$.

The "subprogram" relation ($\Rightarrow$) just defined is reflexive, antisymmetric (i.e., $S_1 \Rightarrow S_2$ does not imply $S_2 \Rightarrow S_1$), and transitive. Therefore it is a partial-ordering relation.

With these definitions, we can now determine the relationship between any programs, with or without state constraints. For instance, consider Programs 2.1 and 2.2 again. Because

$$wp(S_1; /\backslash C; S_2, R) \equiv wp(S_1, C \wedge wp(/\backslash C; S_2, R))$$
$$\equiv wp(S_1, C \wedge wp(S_2, R))$$
$$\equiv wp(S_1, C) \wedge wp(S_1, wp(S_2, R))$$
$$\equiv wp(S_1, C) \wedge wp(S_1; S_2, R),$$

it follows that $wp(S_1;/\backslash C;S_2, R) \supset wp(S_1;S_2, R)$. Thus, by Definition 2.5, Program 2.2 is a subprogram of Program 2.1.

Note that if $C \equiv T$, i.e., if C is always true, then $wp(/\backslash T;S, R) \equiv T \wedge wp(S, R) \equiv wp(S, R)$, and therefore, by Definition 2.4, we get Corollary 2.6.

Corollary 2.6

$/\backslash T; S \Leftrightarrow S.$

That is to say, a state constraint will have no effect on a program if it is always true. On the other hand, if $C \equiv F$, i.e., if C is always false, then $wp(/\backslash F;S, R) \equiv F \wedge wp(S, R) \equiv F \equiv wp(/\backslash F;S', R)$ for any S, S', and R, and therefore we get Corollary 2.7.

Corollary 2.7

$/\backslash F; S \Leftrightarrow /\backslash F; S'.$

In words, any two programs are (trivially) equivalent if both are constrained by a predicate that can never be true.

Although in theory we can insert any constraints anywhere in a program to create a subprogram, it may not serve any purpose at all. The exact nature of constraints, and the points at which they are to be inserted, depend on the purpose to be served.

In the next chapter it is shown how to create simpler subprograms by constraining conditional statements in the program with branch predicates.

State constraints can also be used to prove the correctness of a program. The basic idea involved can be explained as follows. Suppose the function of program S is specified by use of precondition Q and postcondition R. We can construct a new program $/\backslash Q;S;/\backslash R$, which, by definition, is a subprogram of S. This program is defined for any input of S that satisfies Q and that causes R to become true upon an execution of S (if the execution terminates). In other words, $/\backslash Q;S;/\backslash R$ is a subprogram of program S that is correct with respect to precondition Q and postcondition R.

Now let X be the input domain of S, and X′ be the domain for which $/\backslash Q;S;/\backslash R$ is defined. The following possible relationships between X and X′ signify different degrees of correctness of S:

$X \cap X′ = \emptyset$ implies that S will not execute correctly for any input,

$X \supset X′$ implies that S is correct for some inputs,

$X \subseteq X′$ implies that S is correct for all inputs.

For program S to be correct for the entire input domain, X must be a subset of X′, i.e., the following relation must hold:

$$/\backslash Q; S; /\backslash R \Rightarrow S.$$

On the other hand, by definition, the following relation must hold also:

$$S \Rightarrow /\backslash Q; S; /\backslash R.$$

That means the following relation must hold if program S is correct with respect to precondition Q and postcondition R:

$$S \Leftrightarrow /\backslash Q; S; /\backslash R.$$

Path-Oriented Program Analysis

Note that this relation will hold if $S \Leftrightarrow /\backslash Q;S$ and $S \Leftrightarrow S;/\backslash R$. Constraints such as $/\backslash Q$ and $/\backslash R$ here are said to be tautological because they have this property if they are always true at the points where they are located. Thus, to prove the correctness of a program is to preconstrain and postconstrain the program with its preconditions and postconditions, respectively, and then to show that the constraints are tautological. This is described in detail in Chapter 1.

None of the concepts regarding correctness proof discussed here are new. Nevertheless, the preciseness, conciseness, and economy in notation achievable through the use of state constraints are noteworthy.

We do not know of any real programming language that provides a mechanism for implementing state constraints as just defined. Nevertheless, constraint $/\backslash C$ can be simulated by using a statement of the form "`if not C abort`" if we wish to determine through test-execution whether or not a subprogram is defined for a particular input. The execution would abort if it is not.

Appendix A contains some examples of using state constraints to create subprograms in a real program.

3

Subprogram Simplification

Presented in this chapter are three categories of equivalence relations showing how state constraints can be inserted into a program to reduce it to a simpler subprogram. The first indicates how to constrain a program so that the resulting subprogram will have a simpler logical structure; the second shows how the state constraints in a program can be manipulated and simplified. The third shows how to simplify long sequences of assignment statements, which often result from a repeated application of the first two.

The reader will find some of the rules presented in this work trivial and thus unnecessary if the present analysis method is used manually by a programmer. Manual application of the method, however, may prove to be unacceptably error prone or time consuming in certain environments. In that case, a possible solution is to build a software tool to automate the method to the extent possible. These seemingly trivial rules will be useful for that purpose.

Listed below are equivalence relations of the first category, the validity of which is immediately obvious.

Path-Oriented Program Analysis

Corollary 3.1

$/\backslash B;$ **if** B **then** S_1 **else** $S_2 \Leftrightarrow /\backslash B; S_1$.

Proof: By Axiom 2.3,

wp($/\backslash$ B; **if** B **then** S_1 **else** S_2, R)
$\equiv$ B $\wedge$ wp(**if** B **then** S_1 **else** S_2, R)
$\equiv$ B $\wedge$ (B $\wedge$ wp(S_1, R) $\vee$ ¬B $\wedge$ wp(S_2, R))
$\equiv$ B $\wedge$ wp(S_1, R)
$\equiv$ wp($/\backslash$B; S_1, R).   *End of Proof*

Note: Many corollaries and theorems in this book can be simply proved in a similar manner and thus are given without proof.

The meaning of a programming construct, when given in the same font as the main text, is defined as usual. Allowable statements include (but not limited to) those in the following list:

1. assignment statements: x := e, where x is a variable and e is an expression,
2. conditional statements: **if** B **then** S_1 **else** S_2, where S_1 and S_2 are statements, and B is a predicate,
3. repetitive statements: **while** B **do** S or, **repeat** S **until** B, and
4. input–output statements: **read**(x) and **print**(y).

A simple statement is to be delimited by a semicolon (;), and a compound statement by a **begin–end** pair.

When an example program is given in a particular programming language, or when a reference is made to the part thereof, the text is printed in Letter Gothic.

Because we defined the semantics of a state constraint in terms of Dijkstra's weakest preconditions, it is useful to know that, for any deterministic program S and postconditions Q and R, the weakest preconditions wp(S, Q) and wp(S, R) have the following properties:

1. for any S, wp(S, F) $\equiv$ F,
2. for any programming construct S and any predicates Q and R, if Q $\supset$ R then wp(S, Q) $\supset$ wp(S, R),
3. for any programming construct S and any predicates Q and R, (wp(S, Q) $\wedge$ wp(S, R)) $\equiv$ wp(S, Q $\wedge$ R),

4. for any deterministic programming construct S and any predicates Q and R, $(wp(S, Q) \lor wp(S, R)) \equiv wp(S, Q \lor R)$.   *End of Note*

Corollary 3.2

$/\backslash \neg B$; **if** B **then** S_1 **else** $S_2 \Leftrightarrow /\backslash \neg B$; S_2.

Corollary 3.3

$/\backslash B_i$; **if** B_1 **then** S_1 **else if** B_2 **then** S_2 . . . **else if** B_i **then** S_i . . . **else if** B_n **then** $S_n \Leftrightarrow /\backslash \neg B_1 \land \neg B_2 \land . . . \land B_i$; S_i.

Corollary 3.4

$/\backslash B$; **while** B **do** S $\Leftrightarrow /\backslash B$; S; **while** B **do** S.

The usefulness of this corollary will become obvious when we develop another relation later that allows us to move a constraint downstream.

Corollary 3.5

$/\backslash \neg B$; **while** B **do** S $\Leftrightarrow /\backslash \neg B$.

Because S; **while** B **do** S $\Leftrightarrow$ **repeat** S **until** $\neg B$, Corollary 3.4 allows us to write Corollary 3.6.

Corollary 3.6

$/\backslash B$; **while** B **do** S $\Leftrightarrow /\backslash B$; **repeat** S **until** $\neg B$.

Because "**while** B **do** S" is not logically equivalent to "**repeat** S **until** $\neg B$" in general, this shows that $/\backslash C$; $S_1 \Leftrightarrow /\backslash C$; S_2 does not imply $S_1 \Leftrightarrow S_2$ in general.

Examples of how the corollaries just given can be used to create or to simplify subprograms in C++ can be found in Appendix A.

A state constraint not only directly constrains the program state at the point where it is placed, but also indirectly at other points upstream and downstream in control flow as well. Program 2.2 is repeated here for convenience.

Path-Oriented Program Analysis

Program 2.2

$S_1; /\backslash C; S_2$

Note that predicate C is true if and only if $wp(S_1, C)$ is true before execution of S_1. Thus, by constraining the program state between S_1 and S_2 to C, it also indirectly constrains the program state before S_1 to $wp(S_1, C)$, and the program state after S_2 to R, where $wp(S_2, R) \equiv C$.

The *scope* of a state constraint, which is defined to be the range of control flow within which the constraint has an effect, may or may not span the entire program. A state constraint will have no effect beyond a statement that undefines, or assigns a constant value to, the variables involved. For instance, a state constraint like $x > 0$ will have no effect on the program states beyond the statement read(x) upstream, the statement return downstream if x is a local variable, or statement $x := 4$ upstream or downstream.

Because of the scope of a constraint, nonequivalent subprograms may be produced when the same constraint is applied to two functionally equivalent programs. For example, consider the two programs listed below:

```
S₁:  q := 0;
     r := x;
     while r ≥ y do begin r := r − y; q := q + 1 end,
S₂:  q := 0;
     read(x, y);
     r := x;
     while r ≥ y do begin r := r − y; q := q + 1 end
```

Intuitively, we would consider these two programs logically equivalent because both compute the quotient and remainder of doing integer division $x \div y$ in exactly the same way. The only difference is that the input operation is not explicitly specified in S_1. Now if we preconstrain both S_1 and S_2 and write

```
/\x>0; S₁:  /\ x > 0;
            q := 0;
            r := x;
            while r ≥ y do begin r := r − y; q := q + 1 end,
```

$/\backslash x{>}0;\ S_2:\quad /\backslash\ x > 0;$

$\qquad\qquad\quad q := 0;$

$\qquad\qquad\quad$ **read**$(x, y);$

$\qquad\qquad\quad r := x;$

$\qquad\qquad\quad$ **while** $r \geq y$ **do begin** $r := r - y;\ q := q + 1$ **end**

we might think that we have created two equivalent subprograms $/\backslash x >$ $0;\ S_1$ and $/\backslash x > 0;\ S_2$, both of which are defined for positive x only, whereas in fact $/\backslash x > 0;\ S_1$ and $/\backslash x > 0;\ S_2$ are not equivalent. Because the scope of constraint $/\backslash\ x > 0$ is terminated by statement **read**(x, y) in $/\backslash x > 0;\ S_2$, the domain of definition of $/\backslash x > 0;\ S_2$ is in effect not constrained at all, whereas that of $/\backslash x > 0;\ S_1$ is constrained by $/\backslash\ x >$ 0. To constrain S_2 for the same purpose, the constraint has to be inserted immediately following the statement **read**(x, y).

Another view of this property is that exactly the same constraint on the program states in Program 2.2 can be affected by placing constraint $/\backslash wp(S_1, C)$ before S_1 or constraint $/\backslash C$ before S_2. To be more precise, $S_1;/\backslash C;S_2 \Leftrightarrow /\backslash wp(S_1, C);S_1;S_2$ if the scope of $/\backslash C$ is not terminated by S_1. In general, this relationship can be stated as follows.

Theorem 3.7

$S; /\backslash\ R \Leftrightarrow /\backslash Q;S$ if $Q \equiv wp(S, R)$.

This relation can be used repeatedly to move a constraint upstream, i.e., to constrain the program equivalently at a different point upstream.

On the other hand, given a program of the form $/\backslash Q;S$, we can apply the same relation in the other way to move the constraint downstream. In that case, what we need to do is to find a predicate R such that $wp(S, R) \equiv Q$. As discussed in (Huang 1980a), we can do this by letting $R \equiv wp(S^{-1}, Q)$, where S^{-1} is a sequence of statements to be derived from S and Q. By replacing R in $wp(S, R) \equiv Q$, we obtain $wp(S;S^{-1}, Q) \equiv Q$.

Note that if $S;S^{-1}$ is a sequence of assignment statements, $wp(S;S^{-1}, Q) \equiv Q$ is true as long as an execution of $S;S^{-1}$ will not alter the value of any variable that occurs in Q. Thus we may find a suitable S^{-1} by noting that, if S contains a statement that changes the value of a variable in Q, S^{-1} should contain a statement that restores the old value of that variable. The following examples should be helpful in visualizing how to find S^{-1} for given Q and S.

a.
$$Q: \quad x = 100$$
$$S: \quad x := x + 10$$
$$S^{-1}: \quad x := x - 10$$
$$wp(S^{-1}, Q): \quad x = 110$$

b.
$$Q: \quad x > c$$
$$S: \quad x := a$$
$$S^{-1}: \quad \text{(does not exist)}$$
$$wp(S^{-1}, Q): \quad ?$$

c.
$$Q: \quad x > a$$
$$S: \quad \textbf{read}(x)$$
$$S^{-1}: \quad \text{(does not exist)}$$
$$wp(S^{-1}, Q): \quad ?$$

d.
$$Q: \quad x < c$$
$$S: \quad y := y + 1; z := x + y$$
$$S^{-1}: \quad \text{null statement, or "skip"}$$
$$wp(S^{-1}, Q): \quad x < c$$

e.
$$Q: \quad x > a$$
$$S: \quad y := y + 2; w := w + 1; x := x + y$$
$$S^{-1}: \quad x := x - y$$
$$wp(S^{-1}, Q): \quad x > a + y$$

Note that S^{-1} does not exist if S assigns a constant value to a variable in Q as exemplified by cases b and c. The problem of finding S^{-1} becomes more involved whenever S contains a conditional statement or repetitive statement.

From the preceding discussion we see that, for convenience in future applications, Theorem 3.7 has two alternatives.

Theorem 3.7

a. $S;/\backslash R \Leftrightarrow /\backslash wp(S, R);S$, or
b. $/\backslash Q;S \Leftrightarrow S;/\backslash wp(S^{-1}; Q)$.

Now if we apply Theorem 3.7 to a program repeatedly, at some point we would produce a concatenation of two constraints, the meaning of which can be stated as Corollary 3.8.

Corollary 3.8

$$/\backslash C_1;/\backslash C_2;S \Leftrightarrow /\backslash C_1 \wedge C_2;S.$$

This is a direct consequence of Axiom 2.3.

Theorem 3.7 and Corollary 3.8 belong to the second category of equivalence relations that one can use to combine and simplify the constraints placed in a program to make it more readable.

One reason why the state constraints in a program can be simplified is that some state constraints are implied by the others and thus can be eliminated. To be more specific, if two state constraints C_1 and C_2 are such that $C_1 \supset C_2$ then C_2 can be discarded because $C_1 \wedge C_2 \equiv C_1$.

Some state constraints may be eliminated in the simplification process because it is always true because of computation performed by the program. For example, the following program contains such a constraint.

```
x := 0;        ⇔  x := 0;         ⇔  /\0 + 1 ≠ 0   ⇔   x := 0;
y := x + 1;       /\x + 1 ≠ 0;        x := 0;          y := x + 1;
/\y ≠ 0;          y := x + 1;         y := x + 1;
```

Definition 3.9

A state constraint is said to be *tautological* if it can be eliminated without changing the function implemented by the program. To be more precise, the constraint $/\backslash C$ in the program $S_1;/\backslash C; S_2$ is tautological if and only if $S_1;/\backslash C; S_2 \Leftrightarrow S_1;S_2$.

In the preceding paragraph, either S_1 or S_2 may be a null statement. The properties and possible exploitation of tautological constraints are discussed in Chapter 6.

As we might have observed in previous examples, moving state constraints interspersed in the statements to the same point in control flow often leaves a long sequence of assignment statements in the program.

Path-Oriented Program Analysis

These assignment statements may be combined and simplified by using the three equivalence relations presented in the following corollary.

Corollary 3.10

$$x := E_1; x := E_2 \Leftrightarrow x := (E_2)_{E_1 \to x}$$

Here $(E_2)_{E_1 \to x}$ denotes the expression obtained from E_2 by substituting E_1 for every occurrence of x in E_2. For example,

```
x := x + y;    ⇔    x := x + y + 1;
x := x + 1;
```

Although in general two assignment statements cannot be interchanged, an assignment statement may be moved downstream under certain circumstances, in particular, as in Corollary 3.11.

Corollary 3.11

If x_2 does not occur in E_1 then

$$x_1 := E_1; x_2 := E_2 \Leftrightarrow x_2 := (E_2)_{E_1 \to x_1}; x_1 := E_1.$$

For example, we may move the first assignment statement downwards in the program segment,

$$x := x + y;$$
$$z := x + 1;$$

and write

$$z := x + y + 1;$$
$$x := x + y;$$

We may not do the same to the following statements, however,

$$x := x + y;$$
$$y := y + 2;$$

because y, the variable on the left-hand side of the second statement, occurs on the right-hand side of the first statement.

The purpose of an assignment statement is to assign a value to a variable so that it can be used in some statements downstream. Now if the preceding rule is used to move an assignment statement downstream past all statements in which the assigned value is used, the statement becomes redundant and thus can be deleted.

Definition 3.12

A statement in a program is said to be *redundant* if its sole purpose is to define the value of a data structure, and this particular value is not used anywhere in the program.

Obviously a redundant statement can be removed without changing the computation performed by the program.

Corollary 3.13

If $x_1 := E_1; x_2 := E_2$ is a sequence of two assignment statements such that, by interchanging these two statements, $x_1 := E_1$ becomes redundant, then $x_1 := E_1; x_2 := E_2 \Leftrightarrow x_2 := (E_2)_{E_1 \to x_1}$.

In general, Corollary 3.13 becomes applicable when $x_2 := E_2$ is the last statement to make use of definition provided by $x_1 := E_1$. For example,

$$x := x + y \qquad \Leftrightarrow \qquad z := x + y + 1;$$
$$z := x + 1 \qquad\qquad\qquad \text{return z;}$$
$$\text{return z;}$$

Corollaries 3.11 and 3.13 can be used to reduce the number of assignment statements in a program, and thus the number of steps involved in computation. The end result is often a simpler and more understandable program as demonstrated in Example A.1 in Appendix A.

Finally, it should be pointed out that certain sequences of assignment statements can be simplified through symbolic execution and heuristics, but not through the use of Corollaries 3.10, 3.11, and 3.13. For example, consider the following sequence of assignment statements (where "%" denotes a modulus operator):

```
S₁:  r := a % b;
```

Path-Oriented Program Analysis

```
a := b;
b := r;
r := a % b;
a := b;
b := r;
```

We cannot simplify this sequence with the previously mentioned corollaries. Nevertheless, if we perform a symbolic execution of this sequence of statements with the symbolic values: $a \leftarrow A$, $b \leftarrow B$, and $r \leftarrow R$, the net result will be

$$r \leftarrow B\%(A\%B)$$
$$a \leftarrow A\%B$$
$$b \leftarrow B\%(A\%B)$$

Some reflection will show that this result can be produced by using the following sequence of assignment statements:

```
S₂: a := a % b;
    b := b % a;
    r := b;
```

That is to say, the previous S_1 can be reduced to S_2.

4

Program Set

As mentioned before, by inserting a constraint into a program, we shrink the domain for which it is defined. To reverse this process, we need to be able to speak of, and make use of, a set of subprograms. To this end, a new programming construct called a *program set* is now introduced. The meaning of a program set, or a set of programs, is identical to the conventional notion of a set of other objects. As usual, a set of n programs is denoted by $\{P_1, P_2, \ldots, P_n\}$. When used as a programming construct, it describes the computation prescribed by its elements. Formally, the semantics of such a set is defined in Axiom 4.1.

Axiom 4.1

$$wp(\{P_1, P_2, \ldots, P_n\}, R) \equiv wp(P_1, R) \vee wp(P_2, R) \vee \ldots \vee wp(P_n, R).$$

The choice of this particular semantics is explained in detail at the end of this chapter. A program set so defined has all properties commonly found in an ordinary set. For instance, because the logical operation of disjunction is commutative, a direct consequence of Axiom 4.1 is Corollary 4.2.

Corollary 4.2

The ordering of elements in a program set is immaterial, i.e.,

$$\{P_1, P_2\} \Leftrightarrow \{P_2, P_1\}.$$

Furthermore, because every proposition is an idempotent under the operation of disjunction, we have Corollary 4.3.

Corollary 4.3

$P \Leftrightarrow \{P\} \Leftrightarrow \{P, P\}$ for any program P.

In words, a set is unchanged by listing any of its elements more than once. A program set can be used just like a block of statements in program composition. Concatenation of program sets is defined similarly as concatenation of two ordinary sets, in particular, as in Corollary 4.4.

Corollary 4.4

For any programs P, P_1, and P_2,

a. $P;\{P_1, P_2\} \Leftrightarrow \{P;P_1, P;P_2\}$,
b. $\{P_1, P_2\};P \Leftrightarrow \{P_1;P, P_2;P\}$.

Proof: For part a,

$$
\begin{aligned}
wp(P; \{P_1, P_2\}, R) &\equiv wp(P, wp(\{P_1, P_2\}, R)) \\
&\equiv wp(P, wp(P_1, R) \vee wp(P_2, R)) \\
&\equiv wp(P, wp(P_1, R)) \vee wp(P, wp(P_2, R)) \\
&\equiv wp(\{P;P_1, P;P_2\}, R),
\end{aligned}
$$

and hence the proof. Part b can be similarly proved.   *End of Proof*

Subsequently given are a number of useful relations that can be derived from the semantics of a program set.

Corollary 4.5

If $P \Leftrightarrow P'$ then $\{P\} \Leftrightarrow \{P, P'\}$.

Corollary 4.6

If $P \Leftrightarrow P_1$ and $P \Leftrightarrow P_2$ then $P \Leftrightarrow \{P_1, P_2\}$.

In the following corollaries a number of relations that are useful in working with sets of constrained subprograms are presented.

Corollary 4.7

$/\backslash C_1 \vee C_2; P \Leftrightarrow \{/\backslash C_1; P, /\backslash C_2; P\}$.

Proof:

$$wp(/\backslash C_1 \vee C_2; P, R) \equiv (C_1 \vee C_2) \wedge wp(P, R)$$
$$\equiv C_1 \wedge wp(P, R) \vee C_2 \wedge wp(P, R)$$
$$\equiv wp(\{/\backslash C_1; P, /\backslash C_2; P\}, R). \quad \textit{End of Proof}$$

Corollary 4.8

If $C_1, C_2, \ldots, C_n$ are n constraints such that $C_1 \vee C_2 \vee \ldots \vee C_n \equiv T$ then

$$P \Leftrightarrow /\backslash C_1 \vee C_2 \vee \ldots \vee C_n; P \Leftrightarrow \{/\backslash C_1; P, /\backslash C_2; P, \ldots, /\backslash C_n; P\}.$$

The last corollary serves as the basis for decomposing a program into an equivalent set of subprograms. To distinguish this process from the traditional method of decomposing a program into procedures and functions, the present method is called *pathwise decomposition* because the program is divided *along* the control flow, whereas in the traditional method of decomposing a program into procedures and functions, a program is divided *across* the control flow. The concept of pathwise decomposition is discussed in more detail in the next chapter.

There are two more corollaries that we need for discussion in a later chapter.

Path-Oriented Program Analysis

Corollary 4.9

$/\backslash C;\{P_1, P_2\} \Leftrightarrow \{/\backslash C;P_1, /\backslash C;P_2\}.$

Proof:

$$
\begin{aligned}
\mathrm{wp}(/\backslash C; \{P_1, P_2\}, R) &\equiv C \wedge \mathrm{wp}(\{P_1, P_2\}, R) & \textit{(Axiom 2.3)}\\
&\equiv C \wedge(\mathrm{wp}(P_1, R) \vee \mathrm{wp}(P_2, R)) & \textit{(Axiom 4.1)}\\
&\equiv C \wedge\mathrm{wp}(P_1, R) \vee C \wedge \mathrm{wp}(P_2, R)\\
&\equiv \mathrm{wp}(/\backslash C; P_1, R) \vee \mathrm{wp}(/\backslash C; P_2, R)\\
&\equiv \mathrm{wp}(\{/\backslash C; P_1, /\backslash C; P_2\}, R). & \textit{End of Proof}
\end{aligned}
$$

Corollary 4.10

$\{P_1;/\backslash C_1, P_2;/\backslash C_2\} \Leftrightarrow \{P_1;/\backslash C_1, P_2;/\backslash C_2\};/\backslash C_1 \vee C_2.$

Proof:

$$
\begin{aligned}
&\{P_1; /\backslash C_1, P_2; /\backslash C_2\}; /\backslash C_1 \vee C_2\\
\Leftrightarrow\ &\{P_1; /\backslash C_1; /\backslash C_1 \vee C_2, P_2; /\backslash C_2; /\backslash C_1 \vee C_2\} & \textit{(Corollary 4.4)}\\
\Leftrightarrow\ &\{P_1; /\backslash C_1 \vee (C_1 \vee C_2), P_2; /\backslash C_2/\backslash(C_1 \vee C_2)\}\\
\Leftrightarrow\ &\{P_1; /\backslash C_1, P_2; /\backslash C_2\}. & \textit{End of Proof}
\end{aligned}
$$

Because braces and commas may have a different meaning in a real programming language, and because in practice program statements are written line by line from top to bottom, a program set of the form $\{P_1, P_2, \ldots, P_n\}$ may be alternatively written as

```
{{{
      P₁
, , ,
      P₂
, , ,
      .
      .
      .
, , ,
      Pₙ
}}}
```

where triple braces and triple commas are used instead to avoid any possible confusion.

The following example should clarify the concept and notations just introduced:

$$q := 0; r := x;$$
$$\textbf{while } r \geq y \textbf{ do begin } r := r - y; q := q + 1 \textbf{ end}$$
$$\Leftrightarrow q := 0; r := x;$$
$$/ \setminus r \geq y \textbf{ or } r < y;$$
$$\textbf{while } r \geq y \textbf{ do begin } r := r - y; q := q + 1 \textbf{ end}$$
$$\Leftrightarrow q := 0; r := x;$$
$$\{\{\{$$
$$\quad / \setminus r \geq y;$$
$$\quad \textbf{while } r \geq y \textbf{ do begin } r := r - y; q := q + 1 \textbf{ end}$$

$$,,,$$
$$\quad / \setminus r < y;$$
$$\quad \textbf{while } r \geq y \textbf{ do begin } r := r - y; q := q + 1 \textbf{ end}$$
$$\}\}\}$$
$$\Leftrightarrow q := 0; r := x;$$
$$\{\{\{$$
$$\quad / \setminus r \geq y;$$
$$\quad r := r - y; q := q + 1;$$
$$\quad \textbf{while } r \geq y \textbf{ do begin } r := r - y; q := q + 1 \textbf{ end}$$

$$,,,$$
$$\quad / \setminus r < y;$$
$$\}\}\}$$
$$\Leftrightarrow \{\{\{$$
$$\quad q := 0; r := x;$$
$$\quad / \setminus r \geq y;$$
$$\quad r := r - y; q := q + 1;$$
$$\quad \textbf{while } r \geq y \textbf{ do begin } r := r - y; q := q + 1 \textbf{ end}$$

$$,,,$$
$$\quad q := 0; r := x;$$
$$\quad / \setminus r < y;$$
$$\}\}\}$$

Note that a program set may contain elements with overlapping domains of definition. That is, a program set, say, $\{/ \setminus C_1; P_1, / \setminus C_2; P_2, \ldots, / \setminus C_n; P_n\}$, may be constructed in such a way that some inputs may satisfy more than one C_i at the same time. In that case, the program becomes nondeterministic. If an input satisfies C_i and C_j at the same time, we stipulate that either P_i or P_j (but not both) will be chosen to execute. But we cannot tell *a priori* which one will be chosen.

Fortunately we need not to contend with nondeterminism in the present method. The method is intended for real programs. All real programs are deterministic in nature, and all deterministic programs decompose pathwise into deterministic subprograms. Although the definition of program set allows us to create nondeterministic programs, the present method does not require creation or manipulation of nondeterministic programs in its application.

Finally, for those who are familiar with Dijkstra's work on the guarded commands (Dijkstra, 1976), the general form of a program set,

$$\{/ \setminus C_1; P_1, / \setminus C_2; P_2, \ldots, / \setminus C_n; P_n\},$$

may appear to be deceptively similar to Dijkstra's "IF" statement:

$$\textbf{if } C_1 \to P_1 \parallel C_2 \to P_2 \parallel \ldots \parallel C_n \to P_n \textbf{ fi.}$$

Are these two constructs equivalent? Note that, by Axiom 4.1, we have the following corollary:

Corollary 4.11

$$wp(\{/ \setminus C_1; P_1, / \setminus C_2; P_2, \ldots, / \setminus C_n; P_n\}, R)$$
$$\equiv wp(/ \setminus C_1; P_1, R) \vee wp(/ \setminus C_2; P_2, R) \vee \ldots \vee wp(/ \setminus C_n; P_n, R)$$
$$\equiv C_1 \wedge wp(P_1, R) \vee C_2 \wedge wp(P_2, R) \vee \ldots \vee C_n \wedge wp(P_n, R),$$

and, according to the definition given in Dijkstra (1976), we have the following axiom.

Axiom 4.12

$$wp(\textbf{if } C_1 \to P_1 \parallel C_2 \to P_2 \parallel \ldots \parallel C_n \to P_n \textbf{fi}, R)$$
$$\equiv (C_1 \vee C_2 \vee \ldots \vee C_n) \wedge (C_1 \supset wp(P_1, R))$$
$$\wedge (C_2 \supset wp(P_2, R)) \wedge \ldots \wedge (C_n \supset wp(P_n, R)).$$

Therefore, $\{/\backslash C_1;P_1, /\backslash C_2;P_2, \ldots, /\backslash C_n;P_n\}$ is not equivalent to **if** $C_1 \rightarrow P_1 \parallel C_2 \rightarrow P_2 \parallel \ldots \parallel C_n \rightarrow P_n$ **fi** in general.

The reason for choosing the semantics defined by Axiom 4.1 instead of Dijkstra's (i.e., Axiom 4.12) is to make the meaning of a program set as intuitive as possible.

In this book it is appropriate to view a program set as a collection of tools, each of which can be used to do something. As such, if one added a program to the set, one naturally expects the capability of the resulting set to increase, or at least to remain the same.

The capability of a program increases if its weakest precondition becomes weaker for the same postcondition (i.e., the program can do the same for more input data) or if the same set of inputs satisfies a stronger postcondition (i.e., the program can do more computations for the same set of input data).

The semantics specified by Axiom 4.1 conforms to this view of a program set: the larger the set, the more versatile it becomes. In particular, if we added a new program P_2 to the program set $\{P_1\}$ to form the new set $\{P_1, P_2\}$, the weakest precondition of the resulting set becomes $wp(\{P_1, P_2\}, R) \equiv wp(P_1, R) \vee wp(P_2, R)$, which is weaker than (or equivalent to) $wp(\{P_1\}, R)$. This is always true regardless of the relation between P_1 and P_2.

For example, consider the singleton program set $\{/\backslash x > 2; y := 1\}$, which is capable of setting y to 1 if x is greater than 2. If a new program $/\backslash x > 2; y := 2$ is added to this set to form a larger program set $\{/\backslash x > 2; y := 1, /\backslash x > 2; y := 2\}$, then, by Corollary 4.11,

$$wp(\{/\backslash x > 2; y := 1, /\backslash x > 2; y := 2\}, y = 1)$$
$$\equiv x > 2 \vee F \equiv x > 2.$$

That is, the expanded set of programs still has the old capability to set y to 1 if x > 2.

What will happen if we adopt Dijkstra's definition and let the semantics of $\{/\backslash C_1;P_1, /\backslash C_2;P_2, \ldots, /\backslash C_n;P_n\}$ be identical to that of **if** $C_1 \rightarrow P_1 \parallel C_2 \rightarrow P_2 \parallel \ldots \parallel C_n \rightarrow P_n$ **fi**? One immediate consequence is that

$$wp(\{/\backslash C_1; P_1, /\backslash C_2; P_2\}, R)$$
$$\equiv wp(\mathbf{if}\, C_1 \rightarrow P_1 \| C_2 \rightarrow P_2\, \mathbf{fi}, R)$$
$$\equiv (C_1 \vee C_2) \wedge (C_1 \supset wp(P_1, R)) \wedge (C_2 \supset wp(P_2, R))$$

$$\equiv C_1 \wedge \neg C_2 \wedge wp(P_1, R) \vee C_2 \wedge \neg C_1 \wedge wp(P_2, R) \vee C_1 \wedge C_2$$
$$\wedge wp(P_1, R) \wedge wp(P_2, R),$$

and thus

$$wp(/ \backslash x > 2; y := 1, / \backslash x > 2; y := 2, y = 1) \equiv F.$$

That is, by acquiring a new program, the expanded set of programs is no longer capable of setting y to 1 if x is greater than 2. In this book, this is counterintuitive.

There are other fundamental differences between the constrained program $/ \backslash C;P$ and the guarded command $C \rightarrow P$. The former is a compound statement, whereas the latter is only an expression that can be used to construct a statement. The constraint $/ \backslash C$ is introduced as an analysis tool to facilitate analysis of a given program, whereas the guarded command $C \rightarrow P$ is introduced as a synthesis tool to facilitate specification of a program.

It is interesting to note that

$$/ \backslash C; \ \textbf{if } C_1 \rightarrow P_1 \| C_2 \rightarrow P_2 \| \dots \| C_n \rightarrow P_n \textbf{ fi}$$
$$\Leftrightarrow \ \textbf{if } C \wedge C_1 \rightarrow P_1 \| C \wedge C_2 \rightarrow P_2 \| \dots \| C \wedge C_n \rightarrow P_n \textbf{ fi}.$$

5

Pathwise Decomposition

In this chapter we discuss the concept of pathwise decomposition in more detail. First, we need to formally define some terms so that we can speak precisely and concisely.

In abstract, by pathwise decomposition we mean the process of rewriting a program into an equivalent program set, consisting of more than one element. To be more precise, we have the following definition.

Definition 5.1a

Given a piece of source code $/\backslash C;S$, to decompose it *pathwise* is to find a program set $\{/\backslash C_1;S_1, /\backslash C_2;S_2, \ldots, /\backslash C_n;S_n\}$ such that

1. $/\backslash C;S \Leftrightarrow \{/\backslash C_1;S_1, /\backslash C_2;S_2, \ldots, /\backslash C_n;S_n\}$,
2. $n > 1$,
3. $C_i \wedge C_j \equiv F$ for any $i \neq j$, and
4. $C_1 \vee C_2 \vee \ldots \vee C_n. \equiv C$.

Path-Oriented Program Analysis

Presumably, it is written to implement a function that can be decomposed pathwise, as subsequently described.

Definition 5.1b

Given a function, say, f, to decompose it *pathwise* is to rewrite it in such a way that it includes a description of the following elements:

1. $f: X \rightarrow Y$,
2. $f = \{f_1, f_2, \ldots, f_m\}$,
3. $X = X_1 \cup X_2 \cup \ldots \cup X_m$,
4. $f_i: X_i \rightarrow Y$ for all $1 \leq i \leq m$.

Definition 5.2a

A set $\{/ \backslash C_1; S_1, / \backslash C_2; S_2, \ldots, / \backslash C_n; S_n\}$ of subprograms is said to be *compact* if, for any $i \neq j$, $C_i \wedge C_j \equiv F$ implies that S_i is not logically equivalent to S_j.

Intuitively, a program set is said to be compact if every subprogram computes a different function. We can characterize a set of subfunctions in a similar manner.

Definition 5.2b

A set $\{f_1, f_2, \ldots, f_m\}$ of subfunctions is said to be *compact* if, for any $i \neq j$, $X_i \cap X_j = \emptyset$ implies that $f_i \neq f_j$.

Among all the subprograms we can create from a given program, we would be particularly interested in its trace subprograms.

Definition 5.3

A subprogram $/ \backslash C_i; S_i$ (in Definition 5.1a) is said to be a *trace subprogram* (of $/ \backslash C; S$) if execution of the program with any input satisfying C_i will cause the same execution path to be traversed (i.e., S_i contains no branches).

We are interested in trace subprograms because they can be readily obtained. As mentioned previously, the symbolic trace of an execution path is the trace subprogram associated with that path if we treat each true branch predicate on the path as a constraint. That symbolic trace can be produced through static analysis or program instrumentation, as discussed in Chapter 9.

In a way, the compactness of the trace-subprogram set reflects the quality of the source code. Observe that the number of feasible execution paths in a piece of source code is minimal if it has a compact set of trace subprograms. Because the number of execution paths in a program directly contributes to its complexity by certain measures [see, e.g., McCabe (1976)], it is deemed reasonable to use the compactness of the trace-subprogram set as a measure of how well the source code is organized.

Another reason for our interest in trace subprograms is that we can use them to facilitate understanding or to verify the correctness of the program systematically, as follows.

Given a piece of source code $/\backslash C;S$ that implements function f, we first decompose $/\backslash C;S$ pathwise into a set $\{/\backslash C_1;S_1, /\backslash C_2;S_2, \ldots, /\backslash C_n;S_n\}$ of trace subprograms, and then decompose f pathwise into a compact set $\{f_1, f_2, \ldots, f_m\}$ of subfunctions, where $f_j: X_j \to Y$ and $X_j = \{x \mid P_j(x)\}$.

Corollary 5.4

Source code $/\backslash C;S$ implements function f correctly if, for every C_i, $1 \le i \le n$, there exists a predicate P_j, $1 \le j \le m$, such that $X_j = \{x \mid x \in X \land P_j(x)\}$, C_i implies P_j, S_i computes f_j, and $\{x \mid x \in X \land C(x)\}$ is the set of valid inputs to $/\backslash C;S$.

In practice, the applicability of Corollary 5.4, and hence the usefulness of trace subprograms, hinges on n, the number of trace subprograms that exists in the source code. Because the upper bound of the number of paths in the control-flow graph grows exponentially with the number of branches in the program, we may suspect that the number of trace subprograms would be prohibitively large. Fortunately, this is not necessarily so in general. This number has more to do with the number of subdomains envisaged by the program designer than the theoretical upper bound, and thus is more often finite and small enough to make the application of Corollary 5.4 practical.

Path-Oriented Program Analysis

If a loop construct in the source code makes the number of trace subprograms too large to render application of Corollary 5.4 impractical, we may eliminate the problem by treating the loop construct as a single statement, as discussed in the next chapter.

Observe that the subdomains of $/ \backslash C;S$ are defined by C_i's. When the number of inputs that satisfy C_i is reduced to one, it becomes pointless to use Corollary 5.4 to determine its correctness. The reason is that the same result can be obtained through a test-execution, a task that generally requires much less effort.

We subsequently discuss these ideas in more detail.

First, to see how Corollary 5.4 may be used to facilitate understanding of a program, especially those written in a low-level language, consider the source code listed in Program 5.5[1]:

Program 5.5

```
            int i, j, k, flag;
            read (i, j, k);
            if (i ≤ 0) then goto L500;
            if (j ≤ 0) then goto L500;
            if (k ≤ 0) then goto L500;
            flag := 0;
            if (i = j) then flag := flag + 1;
            if (i = k) then flag := flag + 2;
            if (j = k) then flag := flag + 3;
            if (flag ≠ 0) then goto L100;
            if (i + j ≤ k) then goto L500;
            if (j + k ≤ i) then goto L500;
            if (i + k ≤ j) then goto L500;
            flag := 1;
            goto L999;
L100:       if (flag ≠ 1) then goto L200;
            if (i + j ≤ k) then goto L500;
```

---

[1] This is a transliterated version of a legacy program originally written in a primitive language that does not allow the use of logical connectives in prescribing the condition of an "if" statement. The lack of other high-level constructs in this language also made the use of "goto" statements unavoidable.

```
L150:      flag := 2;
           goto L999;
L200:      if (flag ≠ 2) then goto L300;
           if (i + k ≤ j) then goto L500;
           goto L150;
L300:      if (flag ≠ 3) then goto L400;
           if (j + k ≤ i) then goto L500;
           goto L150;
L400:      flag := 3;
           goto L999;
L500:      flag := 4;
L999:      write(flag);
```

This program was written to implement the following specification:

Write a program that takes three integers as input and determine if they could be the lengths of three sides of a triangle, and, if so, indicate the type of triangle formed. To be more specific, the program should read three integers and set a flag as follows:
- *if they form a scalene triangle, then set the flag to 1;*
- *if they form an isosceles triangle then set the flag to 2;*
- *if they form an equilateral triangle then set the flag to 3;*
- *and if they could not form a triangle then set the flag to 4.*

The main idea is that, if we can establish the one-to-one relation between the program components and various components of its specification, we will be able to understand the program or to see its correctness better.

In terms of Definition 5.1b and Corollary 5.4, the function to be computed here is f: $X \rightarrow Y$, where $X = \{<i, j, k> \mid i, j,$ and k are integers$\}$ and $Y = \{1, 2, 3, 4\}$. Function f is decomposed into four subfunctions, i.e., $f = \{f_1, f_2, f_3, f_4\}$ such that f_n: "flag := n", $X_n = \{<i, j, k> \mid i, j,$ k are integers and $P_n(i, j, k)\}$, where

$P_1(i, j, k)$: i, j, and k can form the three sides of a scalene triangle;
$P_2(i, j, k)$: i, j, and k can form the three sides of an isosceles triangle;
$P_3(i, j, k)$: i, j, and k can form the three sides of an equilateral triangle;
$P_4(i, j, k)$: i, j, and k cannot form the three sides of a triangle.

Program 5.5 is in fact correct with respect to the functional specification just given. Many readers, however, may find it difficult to see its correctness because its logical structure is relatively complex.

43

Path-Oriented Program Analysis

The correctness of this program would become much easier to see if we apply Corollary 5.4 to decompose the program pathwise and simplify every trace subprogram to the extent possible. The result is Program 5.6.

Program 5.6

```
int i, j, k, flag;
read (i, j, k);
{{{
    /\ (i≤0)∨(j≤0)∨(k≤0)                                                    // C₁
    flag := 4;                                                              // S₁

    ''''
    /\ (i>0)∧(j>0)∧(k>0)∧(i + j>k)∧(j + k>i)∧(i + k≤j)∧(i≠j)∧(i≠k)∧(j≠k)   // C₂
    flag := 4;                                                              // S₂

    ''''
    /\ (i>0)∧(j>0)∧(k>0)∧(i + j>k)∧(j + k≤i)∧(i≠j)∧(i≠k)∧(j≠k)             // C₃
    flag := 4;                                                              // S₃

    ''''
    /\ (i>0)∧(j>0)∧(k>0)∧(i + j≤k)∧(i≠j)∧(i≠k)∧(j≠k)                       // C₄
    flag := 4;                                                              // S₄

    ''''
    /\ (i>0)∧(j>0)∧(k>0)∧(j + k≤i)∧(i≠j)∧(j = k)                           // C₅
    flag := 4;                                                              // S₅

    ''''
    /\ (i>0)∧(j>0)∧(k>0)∧(i + k≤j)∧(i≠j)∧(i = k)                           // C₆
    flag := 4;                                                              // S₆

    ''''
    /\ (i>0)∧(j>0)∧(k>0)∧(i + j≤k)∧(i = j)∧(i≠k)                           // C₇
    flag := 4;                                                              // S₇

    ''''
    /\ (i>0)∧(j>0)∧(k>0)∧(i = j)∧(i = k)∧(j = k)                           // C₈
    flag := 3;                                                              // S₈

    ''''
    /\ (i>0)∧(j>0)∧(k>0)∧(i + j>k)∧(i = j)∧(i≠k)                           // C₉
    flag := 2;                                                              // S₉

    ''''
    /\ (i>0)∧(j>0)∧(k>0)∧(j + k>i)∧(i≠j)∧(j = k)                           // C₁₀
    flag := 2;                                                              // S₁₀

    ''''
    /\ (i>0)∧(j>0)∧(k>0)∧(i + k>j)∧(i≠j)∧(i = k)                           // C₁₁
    flag := 2;                                                              // S₁₁

    ''''
```

$/\setminus$ (i>0)$\wedge$(j>0)$\wedge$(k>0)$\wedge$(i$\neq$j)$\wedge$(i$\neq$k)$\wedge$(j$\neq$k)$\wedge$(i + j>k)$\wedge$(j + k>i)$\wedge$(i + k>j) $//\ C_{12}$
  flag := 1; $//\ S_{12}$
}}}
write(flag);

In light of Corollary 5.4 we see that

1. C_n implies P_4 and S_n computes f_4 for all n = 1, 2, . . . , 7;
2. C_8 implies P_3 and S_8 computes f_3;
3. C_n implies P_2 and S_n computes f_2 for all n = 9, 10, and 11;
4. C_{12} implies P_1 and S_{12} computes f_1;
5. $C_1 \vee C_2 \vee C_3 \vee C_4 \vee C_5 \vee C_6 \vee C_7 \vee C_8 \vee C_9 \vee C_{10} \vee C_{11} \vee C_{12} \equiv$ T.

Facts 1 through 4 show that Program 5.6, and hence Program 5.5, implements the specification correctly, and Fact 5 shows that all feasible execution paths in Program 5.5 are included in Program 5.6. It is much easier to see the correctness of Program 5.6 because it consists of only 12 simple trace subprograms. The original program (Program 5.5), on the other hand, has a relatively complex logical structure, consisting of 16 "if" statements that require a greater amount of mental efforts to comprehend.

Note that the trace subprogram set in Program 5.6 is not compact. This might not be the making of the original author if there were no restrictions on the syntax of the "if" statements. As shown later in Chapter 7, this program can be rewritten into one that yields a compact set of trace subprograms if the restrictions on syntax are removed.

Most programs contain loop constructs, and loop constructs generally expand into a large number of possible execution paths. Ostensibly, the sheer size of possible execution paths would render the present method completely useless. Fortunately, that is not the case. In practice, many loop constructs would be iterated only for manageably small number of times. And even for those that could be iterated indefinitely, the simplified trace subprograms generated by the first few iterations often shed light on the computation performed by the loop constructs. This is shown in the following with illustrative examples.

First, we use Program A.3 in Appendix A to show that (1) the simplified trace subprograms can be extremely helpful in making the program more understandable, and (2) the number of feasible execution paths in the program is usually much less than its theoretical upper bound.

45

Path-Oriented Program Analysis

Program A.3 is chosen as an example because it is very difficult to understand. The first part of the code is relatively easy to read, but the second (highlighted) part, the part that implements the main function of the program, is not. Very few students in computer science can completely determine what it does in less than 30 minutes.

By use of the present method, the highlighted part of the code can be decomposed pathwise into 10 trace subprograms, as shown in Appendix A. Each trace subprogram is simplified to the extent that the computation it performs becomes self-evident.

Note that the highlighted part of the code includes six "if" statements and three "for" loops. The theoretical upper bound of possible execution paths, therefore, would be far more than $(2^6 =)$ 64. The actual number of feasible execution paths is only 10, a rather manageable number that is much less than the theoretical upper bound.

As explained previously, the present method is intended to be used as follows. Instrument the program for automatic trace-subprogram generation. Select a test case to test-execute the program. As a result, we will be left with the test result and the trace subprogram of the execution path traversed. If the test result is incorrect, we have a fault in the program along the execution path. The trace subprogram can be used to facilitate identification of the fault and selection of additional test cases to exercise the same path if so desired. On the other hand, if the test result is correct, we can simplify and analyze the trace subprogram to determine the computation it performs and the membership of its input domain. Because that same computation is to be performed for all elements in its input domain, a more encompassing conclusion about its correctness can thus be drawn from that test result. This capability is the *raison d'être* of the present method.

It should be remembered, however, that a correct test result does not necessarily imply that the program is correct. A faulty program may produce fortuitously correct results for some inputs. For instance, if an assignment statement such as $x := x + y$ is mistakenly written as $x := x - y$ in the program, the program will produce a correct result if y is given the value of 0 before this statement is executed. In general, this fault should become more obvious in the trace subprogram than in the whole program. This is another reason why it is valuable to generate and analyze the trace subprogram associated with a test-execution.

In some programs, a trace subprogram is defined for only one input. In that case, the value of generating and simplifying trace subprograms becomes suspect, and other provisions of the present method have to be mobilized to solve the problem, as discussed in Chapter 8. The present method, however, explicates the fault if the correctness turns out to be fortuitous.

To illustrate, consider Program A.2. If we execute it with input x = 97, the execution will proceed along the path associated with the trace subprogram, as listed in Program 5.7.

Program 5.7

```
cin >> x;
y = 1;
/\ x <= 100;
x = x + 11;
y = y + 1;
/\!(x <= 100);
/\ y! = 1;
x = x - 10;
y = y - 1;
/\ x <= 100;
x = x + 11;
y = y + 1;
/\!(x <= 100);
/\ y! = 1;
x = x - 10;
y = y - 1;
/\ x <= 100;
x = x + 11;
y = y + 1;
/\!(x <= 100);
/\ y! = 1;
x = x - 10;
y = y - 1;
/\ x <= 100
x = x + 11;
y = y + 1;
```

```
/\!(x <= 100);
/\ y!= 1;
x = x - 10;
y = y - 1;
/\!(x <= 100);
/\!(y!= 1);
z = x - 10;
cout << "z = " << z;
```

This trace subprogram can be simplified to Program 5.8.

Program 5.8

```
cin >> x;
/\ x == 97;
z = 91;
cout << "z = " << z;
```

The simplified trace subprogram (Program 5.8) says that it is defined for the input x = 97 only, and the program should produce 91 as the output. This same conclusion can be reached with less effort by a test-execution. Nevertheless, this analysis result unequivocally indicates that the correctness is not fortuitous.

Knowing that Program 5.7 is a trace subprogram produced by a program with loop constructs, we can obtain a more general result either by (1) analyzing the original program as shown in Example A.2 in Appendix A, or (2) recomposing the loop constructs in the trace subprogram as described in Chapter 7, and then analyzing the recomposed program as explained later. The second approach is preferred because the loop construct recomposed from the simplified trace subprogram is in general simpler than the original.

To see how to construct the trace subprogram associated with an execution path in a program, it is useful to introduce a graphic program-representation scheme.

First, it is explained how the path structures in a directed graph can be described by use of a regular expression.

Briefly, a set of paths between any two nodes in a (directed) graph can be described in terms of symbols associated with the constituent edges as follows. For two edges (labeled by) a and b, we use ab to describe the path formed by connecting a in cascade with b, use $a + b$ to describe the path structure formed by connecting a and b in parallel, and use $a*$ to describe the loop formed by using a, as shown in the following figure:

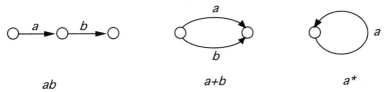

ab   a+b   a*

The same rules also apply to the cases in which a and b are expressions describing complex path structures. Hence a set of paths can be described by an expression composed of edge symbols and three connectives: concatenation, disjunction (+), and looping (*). For example, the set of paths between nodes 1 and 4 in the graph shown in the following figure can be described by the regular expression $a(e+bc*d)$.

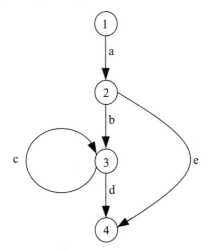

If p describes a path, then $p*$ describes a loop formed by p and hence a set of paths we obtain by iterating the loop for any number of times. Formally,

$$p^* = \lambda + p + pp + ppp + \cdots$$
$$= \sum_{n=0}^{\infty} p^n$$

49

Path-Oriented Program Analysis

where p^n denotes a concatenation of n p's, and $\lambda = p^0$ is a special symbol denoting the identity under the operation of concatenation (i.e., $X\lambda = \lambda X = X$ for any regular expression X) and is to be interpreted as a path of length zero (which we obtain by iterating the loop zero time).

The *program graph* of a program is a directed graph in which each edge is associated with a one-entry–one-exit programming construct.

A cascade of two edges represents a programming construct formed by a sequence (concatenation) of two components, as depicted in the following figure.

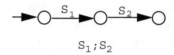

$$S_1 ; S_2$$

Two edges are connected in parallel to represent the program set consisting of the associated components, as shown in the following figure.

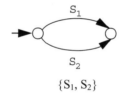

$$\{S_1, S_2\}$$

A conditional statement of the form **if** B **then** S_1 **else** S_2 therefore can be represented by the program graph shown in the following figure because it is logically equivalent to the program set $\{/\backslash B;S_1, /\backslash \neg B;S_2\}$.

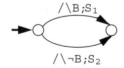

if B **then** S_1 **else** S_2

A loop formed by an edge associated with programming construct S is used to represent a program set whose elements are all possible concatenations of S.

S

S*

To be more specific, S* is defined as

$$S^* \Leftrightarrow \{\lambda, \ S, \ S; S, \ S; S; S, \ S; S; S; S, \ \ldots\}$$

$$\Leftrightarrow \bigcup_{n=0}^{\infty} S^n$$

where S^n denotes a concatenation of n S's, and λ ($= S^0$) is the identity under the operation of concatenation, i.e., a special programming construct having the property that $\lambda; S \Leftrightarrow S; \lambda \Leftrightarrow S$ for any S. It corresponds to a null statement or a NO-OP operation in a machine code.

A loop construct of the form **while B do** S can thus be represented by the program graph in the following figure,

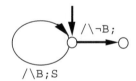

while B do S

and by expression $(/ \backslash B; S)^*; / \backslash \neg B$ in the language of regular expressions.

For example, consider the following program:

```
read(a, b, c);
w := b − a;
while (w > e)
    begin
        p := a + w / 3;
        u := f(p);
        q := b − w / 3;
        v := f(q);
        if (u < v)
            a := p;
```

```
        else
            b := q;
        w := b − a
      end;
    max := (a + b) / 2;
    print (max);
```

According to the graphic representation scheme just described, this program can be represented by the following program graph:

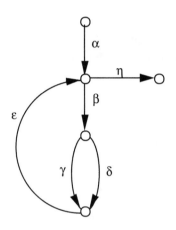

where   α: **read** (a, b, c);
                     w := b − a;
        β: / \ w > e;
                     p := a + w / 3;
                     u := f(p);
                     q := b − w / 3;
                     v := f(q);
        γ: / \ u ≥ v;
                     b := q;
        δ: / \ u < v;
                     a := p;
        ε: w := b − a;
        η: / \ w ≤ e;
                     max := (a + b) / 2;
                     print(max);

Because the paths in a graph can be described by a regular expression over the symbols assigned to each edge, we can now speak of the trace subprograms $\alpha\beta\gamma\epsilon\eta$, $\alpha\beta\delta\epsilon\eta$, $\alpha\beta\delta\epsilon\beta\delta\epsilon\eta$, and so on. Furthermore, we can refer to the program set $\{\alpha\beta\gamma\epsilon\eta, \alpha\beta\delta\epsilon\eta\}$ succinctly in regular expression as $\alpha\beta(\gamma + \delta)\epsilon\eta$, and the entire program as $\alpha(\beta(\gamma + \delta)\epsilon)^*\eta$ (the set of all paths from the entry to the exit). This graphic representation scheme allows us to speak of the various trace subprograms precisely and concisely, and to see how they relate to one another. Some paths included in the set described by $\alpha(\beta(\gamma + \delta)\epsilon)^*\eta$ will be infeasible execution paths. The trace subprogram associated with an infeasible path will have an empty input domain.

The use of the program graphs previously described allows us to generalize the applicability of the present analysis method. All we need to do is to describe the execution path to be analyzed in a program graph. The program in question could be written in any language with any paradigm, and the execution path could span more than one program unit.

The discussion so far, however, is limited to path structures describable by a regular expression involving no star operations. We can learn more about what a piece of source code does if we can analyze path structures involving star operations (i.e., involving implicit or explicit loop constructs) as well. This is discussed in the next chapter.

6

Tautological Constraints

As demonstrated in the preceding chapters, inserting certain state constraints into a program often allows the resulting program to be simplified. The program so produced, however, is in general a subprogram of the original program. To simplify a program, therefore, one needs to simplify a set of its subprograms, and then recompose the program from the simplified subprograms. Now, if the inserted constraint is tautological (see Definition 3.9), the resulting program is equivalent to the original. Therefore, we may be able to simplify a program directly by using tautological constraints. The ability to find tautological constraints is important in that, when we work with a loop construct, we often need to find its loop invariants that may allow us to simplify the loop body. Because a loop invariant is a condition that is true just before the loop is entered, the tautological constraints that immediately precede the loop construct often give us the clues as to what might be the invariant of that loop. Subsequently given is a set of relations that can be used for this purpose.

Path-Oriented Program Analysis

Corollary 6.1

$$/\backslash Q;\ x := E \Leftrightarrow /\backslash Q;\ x := E;/\backslash (Q' \wedge x = E')_{x' \to E}{}^{-1}$$

where $(Q' \wedge x = E')_{x' \to E}{}^{-1}$ is a predicate we construct by following the subsequent steps:

We obtain Q' and E' from Q and E, respectively, by replacing every occurrence of x with x', and then replacing every occurrence of x' with E^{-1}. E^{-1} is an expression we obtain by solving the equation $x = E'$ for x' such that $x' = E^{-1}$.

To be more specific, given a predicate Q and an assignment statement of the form $x := E$, the strongest postcondition $sp(Q, x := E)$ can be constructed as follows:

1. Write $Q \wedge x = E$.
2. Replace every occurrence of x in Q and E with x' to yield $Q' \wedge x = E'$.
3. If x' occurs in E', then construct $x' = E^{-1}$ from $x = E'$ such that $x = E' \equiv x' = E^{-1}$ (i.e., solve the equation $x = E'$ for x'); otherwise E^{-1} does not exist.
   If E^{-1} exists, replace every occurrence of x' in $Q' \wedge x = E'$ with E^{-1}. Otherwise, replace every atomic predicate in $Q' \wedge x = E'$ having at least one occurrence of x' with T (the constant predicate TRUE).

The following examples should clarify the steps just described.

Q	x := E	$(Q' \wedge x = E')_{x' \to E}{}^{-1}$,	which can be simplified to
$x = 0$	$x := 10$	$T \wedge x = 10$	$x = 10$
$a > 1$	$x := 1$	$a > 1 \wedge x = 1$	$a > 1 \wedge x = 1$
$x < 10$	$x := x + 1$	$x - 1 < 10$	$x < 11$
$x \neq y$	$x := x - y$	$x + y \neq y$	$x \neq 0$

For a conditional statement we have the following corollary.

Corollary 6.2

$/\backslash C;$ if B then S_1 else $S_2 \Leftrightarrow /\backslash C;$ if B then S_1 else $S_2;/\backslash (R_1 \vee R_2)$ if $/\backslash C \wedge B; S_1 \Leftrightarrow /\backslash C \wedge B; S_1;/\backslash R_1$ and $/\backslash C \wedge \neg B; S_2 \Leftrightarrow /\backslash C \wedge \neg B; S_2;/\backslash R_2$.

For example, let $C \equiv a \neq b$, $B \equiv a > b$, $S_1 \Leftrightarrow a := a - b$, and $S_2 \Leftrightarrow b := b - a$. Then

$$/\backslash a \neq b \wedge a > b; a := a - b \Leftrightarrow /\backslash a \neq b \wedge a > b;$$
$$a := a - b; /\backslash a > 0 \qquad\qquad (by\ 6.1)$$

$$/\backslash a \neq b \wedge a \leq b; b := b - a \Leftrightarrow /\backslash a \neq b \wedge a \leq b;$$
$$b := b - a; /\backslash b > 0 \qquad\qquad (by\ 6.1)$$

Thus, by Corollary 6.2, we have

$$/\backslash a \neq b;\ \textbf{if } a > b \textbf{ then } a := a - b \textbf{ else } b := b - a$$
$$\Leftrightarrow\quad /\backslash a \neq b;\ \textbf{if then } a := a - b \textbf{ else } b := b - a; /\backslash (a > 0 \vee b > 0),$$

For loop constructs, we have the following corollaries.

Corollary 6.3

a. **while B do S** $\Leftrightarrow$ **while B do S;**$/\backslash \neg B$.
b. **repeat S until** $\neg B \Leftrightarrow$ **repeat S until** $\neg B;/\backslash \neg B$.

These are the direct consequence of the semantics of the loop constructs.

Corollary 6.4

$/\backslash C;$**while B do S** $\Leftrightarrow /\backslash C;$**while B do S;**$/\backslash C$ if wp(S, C) $\equiv$ C.

This corollary says that, if an execution of S, the loop body, does not affect the truth value of C in any way then we can postconstrain the construct with C.

Theorem 6.5

$/\backslash C;$**while B do S** $\Leftrightarrow /\backslash C;$**while B do S;**$/\backslash P$

if $L = \{(x_1, x_2, \ldots, x_n) | P(x_1, x_2, \ldots, x_n)\}$,

Path-Oriented Program Analysis

where $x_1, x_2, \ldots, x_n$ are the variables involved in S, and L is the set of n-tuples of values assumable by these variables upon an execution of the loop construct **while B do** S. The predicate $P(x_1, x_2, \ldots, x_n)$ defines L as a subset of the product set $X_1 \times X_2 \times \ldots \times X_n$, where X_i is the domain of x_i for all $1 \le i \le n$.

The membership of L is recursively defined by the program as follows.

1. $(a_1, a_2, \ldots, a_n) \in L$.
2. If $(x_1, x_2, \ldots, x_n) \in L \land B$, then $S(x_1, x_2, \ldots, x_n) \in L$.

The initial element $(a_1, a_2, \ldots, a_n)$ is specified in the constraint C, and $S(x_1, x_2, \ldots, x_n)$ denotes a new n-tuple we obtain by executing S with $(x_1, x_2, \ldots, x_n)$ as the initial state.

For convenience, we call $x_1, x_2, \ldots, x_n$ the *active variables*, and L the *intrinsic set*, of the loop construct **while B do** S.

To illustrate, consider this program:

$$x := 1;$$
$$\textbf{while } x \ne 10 \textbf{ do } x := x + 2;$$

$$\Leftrightarrow x := 1;$$
$$/\backslash x = 1;$$
$$\textbf{while } x \ne 10 \textbf{ do } x := x + 2;$$

The intrinsic set of this loop construct is a set of integers recursively defined as follows.

1. $1 \in L$.
2. If $x \in L$ and $x \ne 10$ then $x + 2 \in L$.

This definition essentially consists of two rules that can be used to generate all the elements in the set. Obviously, these two rules generate all odd integers greater than or equal to 1. In the standard subset notation this set can be described as $L = \{x \mid x \ge 1 \text{ and } odd(x)\}$. Thus,

$$x := 1; \textbf{ while } x \ne 10 \textbf{ do } x := x + 2$$
$$\Leftrightarrow x := 1; \textbf{ while } x \ne 10 \textbf{ do } x := x + 2; /\backslash x = 10 \qquad (by\ 6.3)$$
$$\Leftrightarrow x := 1; /\backslash x = 1; \textbf{ while } x \ne 10 \textbf{ do } x := x + 2;$$
$$/\backslash x = 10 \qquad (by\ 6.1)$$
$$\Leftrightarrow x := 1; /\backslash x = 1; \textbf{ while } x \ne 10 \textbf{ do } x := x + 2;$$
$$/\backslash (x \ge 1 \land odd(x)); /\backslash x = 10 \qquad (by\ 6.5)$$

$\Leftrightarrow$ x := 1; /\x = 1; while x $\neq$ 10 do x := x + 2;
   /\(x $\geq$ 1 $\wedge$ *odd*(x) $\wedge$ x = 10)
$\Leftrightarrow$ x := 1/\x = 1; while x $\neq$ 10 do x := x + 2; /\F,

indicating that the loop will not terminate because it is postconstrained by F.

To illustrate further, consider the following program:

q := 0; r := x;
while r $\geq$ y do begin r := r $-$ y; q := q + 1 end

First, we observe that

$$q := 0; r := x \Leftrightarrow q := 0; r := x; /\q = 0 \wedge r = x \qquad (by\ 6.1)$$

and for the loop construct

/\q = 0 $\wedge$ r = x; while r $\geq$ y do begin r := r $-$ y;
   q := q + 1 end

the loop body clearly indicates that the loop intrinsic set is a set of pairs of the form (r, q) recursively defined as follows:

1. (x, 0) $\in$ L.
2. If (r, q) $\in$ L then (r $-$ y, q+1) $\in$ L.

In general, we can translate a recursive definition of this sort by generating a number of elements in the set until we can see the pattern clear enough to guess its definition in the standard subset notation. We can then prove the correctness of the guess by using mathematical induction.

In this case, L can be described in the standard subset notation as

$$L = \{(r, q)|P(r, q)\} = \{(r, q)|r = x - q \times y \wedge q \geq 0\}.$$

Hence, we have

/\q = 0 $\wedge$ r = x; while r $\geq$ y do begin r := r $-$ y;
   q := q + 1 end
$\Leftrightarrow$ /\q = 0 $\wedge$ r = x; while r $\geq$ y do begin r := r $-$ y;
   q := q + 1 end;
   /\r = x $-$ q $\times$ y $\wedge$ q $\geq$ 0 $(by\ 6.5)$
$\Leftrightarrow$ /\q = 0 $\wedge$ r = x; while r $\geq$ y do begin r := r $-$ y;
   q := q + 1 end;
   /\r = x $-$ q $\times$ y $\wedge$ q $\geq$ 0 $\wedge$ r < y. $(by\ 6.3)$

59

Path-Oriented Program Analysis

As explained previously, the preceding constitutes a proof that $T\{q := 0 \wedge r := x; \textbf{while } r \geq y \textbf{ do begin } r := r - y; q := q + 1 \textbf{ end}\}r = x - q \times y \wedge q \geq 0 \wedge r < y$, i.e., the program will perform the integer division $x \div y$ to produce the quotient q and remainder r.

A few more substantial examples follow.

Example: The function GCD (greatest common divisor) has the following properties:

$$GCD(a, b) = GCD(a-b, b) \text{ if } a > b, \quad (1)$$
$$GCD(a, b) = GCD(a, b-a) \text{ if } a < b, \quad (2)$$
$$GCD(a, b) = a = b \text{ if } a = b. \quad (3)$$

Now, consider the following program for computing GCD(x, y) for any pair of positive integers x and y:

```
/\x > 0 ∧ y > 0;
a := x;
b := y;
while a ≠ b do begin if a > b then a := a − b
else b := b − a end;
```

The active variables of the while loop are a and b. L, the intrinsic set of this loop, is a set of pairs recursively defined as follows:

1. $(x, y) \in L$.
2. If $(a, b) \in L \wedge a \neq b$, and if $a > b$ then $(a-b, b) \in L$, else if $a \leq b$ then $(a, b-a) \in L$.

L can be described in the standard subset notation:

$$L = \{(a, b) \mid GCD(a, b) = GCD(x, y)\}.$$

For example, if $x = 21$ and $y = 6$, $GCD(21, 6) = GCD(15, 6) = GCD(9, 6) = GCD(3, 6) = GCD(3, 3)$. Thus the intrinsic set L is $\{(21, 6), (15, 6), (9, 6), (3, 6), (3, 3)\}$.

Obviously, according to Corollary 6.1, we have

$$\wedge \ x > 0 \wedge y > 0; a := x; b := y;$$
$$\Leftrightarrow \ \wedge \ x > 0 \wedge y > 0; a := x; b := y; \wedge a > 0 \wedge b > 0;$$

For the loop construct, we have

$/\!\!\backslash$ a > 0 $\wedge$ b > 0; **while** a $\neq$ b **do begin if** a > b **then** a: $=$ a $-$ b
    else b := b $-$ a **end**;
$\Leftrightarrow$ $/\!\!\backslash$ a > 0 $\wedge$ b > 0; **while** a $\neq$ b **do begin if** a > b **then** a := a $-$ b
    else b := b $-$ a **end**;
  $/\!\!\backslash$ a $=$ b;   *(by 6.3)*
$\Leftrightarrow$ $/\!\!\backslash$ a > 0 $\wedge$ b > 0; **while** a $\neq$ b **do begin if** a > b **then** a := a $-$ b
    else b := b $-$ a **end**;
  $/\!\!\backslash$ a $=$ b $\wedge$ GCD(a, b) $=$ GCD(x, y);   *(by 6.5)*
$\Leftrightarrow$ $/\!\!\backslash$ a > 0 $\wedge$ b > 0; **while** a $\neq$ b **do begin if** a > b **then** a := a $-$ b
    else b := b $-$ a **end**;
  $/\!\!\backslash$ a $=$ b $=$ GCD(x, y);   *[by Property (3)]*

Example: The following list is a program for computing a^b:

```
x := a;
y := b;
z := 1;
while y ≠ 0 do
        begin
                if (y ÷ 2) × 2 ≠ y then z := z × x;
                y := y ÷ 2;
                x := x × x;
        end;
```

The loop intrinsic set is a set of triples of integers and can be recursively defined as follows:

1. $(a, b, 1) \in L$.
2. If $(x, y, z) \in L$ and $y \neq 0$ then $(x^2, y \div 2, z \times x^{rem(y,\,2)}) \in L$.

In the preceding definition, *rem*(y, 2) denotes the remainder of dividing y by 2. The central problem here is to define the loop intrinsic set in the standard subset notation. In this case, a possible definition is

$$L = \{(x, y, z) \mid x^y z = a^b \text{ and } x = a^{2^n}$$
    and n is a nonnegative integer}.

Thus, by Corollary 6.3 and Theorem 6.5, we can tautologically postconstrain the loop construct with $y = 0 \wedge x^y z = a^b \wedge x = a^{2^n} \wedge n \geq 0$, which implies $z = a^b$.

Path-Oriented Program Analysis

The significance of Theorem 6.5 can now be explained as follows. In general, a loop construct embodies the recursive definition of some set, say, A. Now, if we can redefine A in the form $\{a \mid P(a)\}$ then we can postconstrain the loop construct with P tautologically. Thus, if we can find a systematic method to translate the recursive definition of a set into an equivalent definition of the form $\{a \mid P(a)\}$ then we have a systematic method to prove the correctness of a loop construct! The interested reader should search the literature to see if such a method exists.

The following sections present some more relations that may be useful in dealing with loop constructs.

Corollary 6.6

a. **while B do S $\Leftrightarrow$ while B do begin $/\backslash$B; S end,**
b. $/\backslash$B; **repeat S until $\neg$B $\Leftrightarrow$ $/\backslash$B; repeat $/\backslash$B; S until $\neg$B.**

Part a says that the semantics of this loop will remain the same if we preconstrain the loop body with B because S will never be executed unless B is true. Part b is different because, unless the repeat statement is preconstrained by B, S will be executed at least once even if B is false when the loop is entered.

Theorem 6.7

If $(Q \wedge B) \supset wp(S, Q)$ then

a. $/\backslash$Q; **while B do S $\Leftrightarrow$ $/\backslash$Q; while B do begin S;$/\backslash$Q end.**
b. $/\backslash$Q; **while B do S $\Leftrightarrow$ $/\backslash$Q; while B do begin $/\backslash$Q;S end.**

This theorem says that, if Q is a loop invariant, we can postconstrain or preconstrain the loop body with Q without changing its semantics. This follows directly from the definition of a loop invariant.

The converse of this theorem is also true and useful. That is, if we found that a while loop is tautologically preconstrained with Q, we determine if the loop body is tautologically constrained by the same. If so, we can conclude that Q is a loop invariant.

Theorem 6.8

If C ⊃ wp(S, Q) and (Q ∧ B) ⊃ wp(S, Q), then

    a. $/\backslash$C; **repeat S until** ¬B ⇔ $/\backslash$C; **repeat** $/\backslash$Q;S **until** ¬B,
    b. $/\backslash$C; **repeat S until** ¬B ⇔ $/\backslash$C; **repeat** S;$/\backslash$Q **until** ¬B.

This theorem is Theorem 6.7 tailored for repeat loops (Huang, 1980a).

Theorem 6.9

If wp(S^{-1}, B) ≡ R then

    a. $/\backslash$B; **while B do S** ⇔ $/\backslash$B; **while B do** S; $/\backslash$R,
    b. $/\backslash$B; **repeat S until** ¬B ⇔ $/\backslash$B; **repeat** S **until** ¬B; $/\backslash$R.

The predicate R in this theorem is the loop predicate B modified by an execution of S. This theorem says that, if we know the loop will be iterated at least once, and B is true before the loop is entered, then we can postconstrain the loop with R. For instance, consider the following construct:

```
/\ x ≤ 100;
while (x ≤ 100)
    begin
        x := x + 11;
        y := y + 1;
    end;
```

After an execution of x := x + 11; y := y + 1, the condition x ≤ 100 becomes x ≤ 111. Therefore we can postconstrain this construct with x ≤ 111 without changing its semantics. That is,

```
/\ x ≤ 100;
while (x ≤ 100)
    begin
        x := x + 11;
        y := y + 1;
```

```
         end;
    ⇔    /\ x ≤ 100;
         while (x ≤ 100)
             begin
                 x := x + 11;
                 y := y + 1;
             end;
             /\ x ≤ 111;
```

Recall that the loop invariant of a while loop is defined to be a condition that is true before the loop is entered and is true after every subsequent iteration of the loop. For some constructs, however, it is possible to have a condition that is not true at the entry but is true after every iteration of the loop body. Subsequently given is an example of such a construct. The condition $y \neq 1$ is not true at the entry of the loop. Nevertheless it becomes always true after the first iteration:

```
    /\ y = 1;
    /\ x ≤ 100;
    while (x ≤ 100)
        begin
            x := x + 11;
            y := y + 1;
        end;
```

For such constructs we have the following theorem.

Theorem 6.10

If $wp(S^{-1}, C) \equiv Q$ and $(Q \wedge B) \supset wp(S, Q)$ then

$$/\backslash C;/\backslash B;\textbf{while B do S} \Leftrightarrow /\backslash C;/\backslash B;\textbf{while B do S}; /\backslash Q.$$

In effect, this theorem says that if a "while" loop will be iterated at least once, and if some condition Q becomes the loop invariant after the first iteration, then this loop can be postconstrained by Q without changing its semantics.

Corollary 6.11

$/\backslash$B; while B do begin S; $/\backslash$C end

$\Leftrightarrow /\backslash$B; S; while B do begin $/\backslash$C; S end; $/\backslash$C.

Corollary 6.12

$/\backslash$C; repeat S; $/\backslash$C until ¬B $\Leftrightarrow /\backslash$C; repeat $/\backslash$C;
   S until ¬B; $/\backslash$C.

Finally, the semantics of a program will not be changed by inserting into it a new constraint that is implied by an adjacent constraint, i.e., Corollary 6.13.

Corollary 6.13

$/\backslash C_1$; S $\Leftrightarrow /\backslash C_1$; $/\backslash C_2$; S if $C_1 \supset C_2$.

The utility of these relations is further demonstrated in Appendix A by their application to Program A.2.1 to obtain the following result.

Program A.2.1

```
cin >> x;
y = 1;
/\ x <= 100;
while (x <= 100) {
    x = x + 11;
    y = y + 1;
}
while (y != 1) {
    x = x - 10;
    y = y - 1;
    while (x <= 100) {
        x = x + 11;
        y = y + 1;
    }
}
```

```
cout << "z = " << z << endl;

⇔ cin >> x;
y = 1;
/\ x <= 100;
while (x <= 100) {
    x = x + 11;
    y = y + 1;
}
while (y != 1) {
    {{{
        /\ x <= 110;
        x = x + 1;
    ...
        /\ x > 110;
        x = x - 10;
        y = y - 1;
    }}}
}
cout << "z = " << z << endl;
```

Tautological constraints in a program allow us to simplify or to transform the program. Therefore, as a general rule, we start by inserting as many tautological constraints into the part of the source code being examined. We then apply appropriate rules to rewrite the program. Once the rules have been applied, the tautological constraints will no longer be needed, and therefore can be discarded. For this reason, it is useful to mark a tautological constraint in some way. In this book tautological constraints are printed in italic.

We may alleviate difficulty in understanding a loop construct by finding as many tautological constraints as possible at the three points in the control flow: one just before the loop is entered, another at the end of the loop body, and yet another immediately after the loop is terminated. These tautological constraints tend to give strong hints about possible candidates for the loop invariant. Once the invariant is found, the understanding becomes easier.

More examples can be found in Appendix A. Note that in Examples A.1 and A.2, to make it easier to follow the steps taken in analysis, a pair of program texts is listed side by side to show what is done in each step. One or more rules could be applied to the statements on the left-hand side. Arrows on the left margin mark the statements directly involved. The resulting text is listed on the right-hand side, with all added or altered statements printed in boldface type, and deleted statements are stricken through. Each pair is followed by an explanation of the rules used and the rationale behind that step, if appropriate. The text on the right-hand side is then copied to the left-hand side of the next pair to become the source of the next step.

7

Program Recomposition

We now turn to address the question of how to recompose a program from its subprograms. Recomposition of a loopless program is relatively easy. Subsequently given are two relations that can be used for that purpose.

Corollary 7.1

if B **then** S_1 **else** S_2; $\Leftrightarrow \{/ \setminus B; S_1, / \setminus \neg B; S_2\}$.

Corollary 7.2

$$
\begin{array}{ll}
\textbf{if } B \textbf{ then } S_1 & \Leftrightarrow \{\{\{ \\
\textbf{else if } B_2 \textbf{ then } S_2 & \quad / \setminus B_1; \\
\qquad . & \quad S_1; \\
\qquad . & \\
\qquad . & ,,, \\
& \quad / \setminus \neg B_1 \wedge B_2; \\
\textbf{else if } B_n \textbf{ then } S_n & \quad S_2; \\
\textbf{else } S_{n+1}; & ,,,
\end{array}
$$

$$.$$
$$.$$
$$.$$

,,,
$$/\backslash \; \neg B_1 \wedge \neg B_2 \wedge \ldots \wedge \neg B_{n-1} \wedge B_n;$$
$$S_n;$$

,,,
$$/\backslash \; \neg B_1 \wedge \neg B_2 \wedge \ldots \wedge \neg B_n;$$
$$S_{n+1};$$
$$\}\}\}$$

For example, Corollary 7.2 can be applied to recompose Program 5.5 from the simplified subprograms in Program 5.6, which is now repeated for reference.

Program 5.6

```
int  i, j, k, flag;
read (i, j, k);
{{{
        /\ (i≤0)∨(j≤0)∨(k≤0);
        flag : = 4;

,,,
        /\ (i>0)∧(j>0)∧(k>0)∧(i+j>k)∧(j+k>i)
           ∧(i+k≤j)∧(i≠j)∧(i≠k)∧(j≠k);
        flag : = 4;

,,,
        /\ (i>0)∧(j>0)∧(k>0)∧(i+j>k)∧(j+k≤i)
           ∧(i≠j)∧(i≠k)∧(j≠k);
        flag : = 4;

,,,
        /\ (i>0)∧(j>0)∧(k>0)∧(i+j≤k)∧(i≠j)
           ∧(i≠k)∧(j≠k);
        flag : = 4;

,,,
        /\ (i>0)∧(j>0)∧(k>0)∧(j+k≤i)∧(i≠j)∧(j = k);
        flag : = 4;

,,,
```

```
        / \ (i>0)∧(j>0)∧(k>0)∧(i+k≤j)∧(i≠j)∧(i=k);
        flag := 4;
  """
        / \ (i>0)∧(j>0)∧(k>0)∧(i+j≤k)∧(i=j)∧(i≠k);
        flag := 4;
  """
        / \ (i>0)∧(j>0)∧(k>0)∧(i=j)∧(i=k)∧(j=k);
        flag := 3;
  """
        / \ (i>0)∧(j>0)∧(k>0)∧(i+j>k)∧(i=j)∧(i≠k);
        flag := 2;
  """
        / \ (i>0)∧(j>0)∧(k>0)∧(j+k>i)∧(i≠j)∧(j=k);
        flag := 2;
  """
        / \ (i>0)∧(j>0)∧(k>0)∧(i+k>j)∧(i≠j)∧(i=k);
        flag := 2;
  """
        / \ (i>0)∧(j>0)∧(k>0)∧(i≠j)∧(i≠k)∧(j≠k)
              ∧(i+j>k)∧(j+k>i)∧(i+k>j);
        flag := 1;
}}}
write(flag);
```

To simplify the state constraints associated with these subprograms, it is useful to let

A_i: $i \leq 0$,
A_j: $j \leq 0$,
A_k: $k \leq 0$,
B_{ij}: $i + j \leq k$,
B_{jk}: $j + k \leq i$,
B_{ki}: $k + i \leq j$,
C_{ij}: $i = j$,
C_{jk}: $j = k$,
C_{ki}: $k = i$.

Path-Oriented Program Analysis

Note that the following relations can also be used to simplify the state constraints:

$$\neg A_i \wedge \neg A_j \wedge \neg A_k \wedge B_{ij} \supset \neg C_{jk} \wedge \neg C_{ki}$$
$$\neg A_i \wedge \neg A_j \wedge \neg A_k \wedge B_{jk} \supset \neg C_{ij} \wedge \neg C_{ki}$$
$$\neg A_i \wedge \neg A_j \wedge \neg A_k \wedge B_{ki} \supset \neg C_{ij} \wedge \neg C_{jk}$$

$$\neg A_i \wedge \neg A_j \wedge \neg A_k \wedge C_{ij} \supset \neg B_{jk}$$
$$\neg A_i \wedge \neg A_j \wedge \neg A_k \wedge C_{ij} \supset \neg B_{ki}$$
$$\neg A_i \wedge \neg A_j \wedge \neg A_k \wedge C_{jk} \supset \neg B_{ij}$$
$$\neg A_i \wedge \neg A_j \wedge \neg A_k \wedge C_{jk} \supset \neg B_{ki}$$
$$\neg A_i \wedge \neg A_j \wedge \neg A_k \wedge C_{ki} \supset \neg B_{ij}$$
$$\neg A_i \wedge \neg A_j \wedge \neg A_k \wedge C_{ki} \supset \neg B_{jk}$$

$$C_{ij} \wedge \neg C_{jk} \equiv C_{ij} \wedge \neg C_{ki}$$
$$C_{jk} \wedge \neg C_{ki} \equiv C_{jk} \wedge \neg C_{ij}$$
$$C_{ki} \wedge \neg C_{ij} \equiv C_{ki} \wedge \neg C_{jk}$$

For the subprograms that compute flag $:= 4$ we have

$$A_i \vee A_j \vee A_k$$
$$\vee \neg A_i \wedge \neg A_j \wedge \neg A_k \wedge \neg B_{ij} \wedge \neg B_{jk} \wedge B_{ki} \wedge \neg C_{ij} \wedge \neg C_{jk} \wedge \neg C_{ki}$$
$$\vee \neg A_i \wedge \neg A_j \wedge \neg A_k \wedge \neg B_{ij} \wedge B_{jk} \wedge \neg C_{ij} \wedge \neg C_{jk} \wedge \neg C_{ki}$$
$$\vee \neg A_i \wedge \neg A_j \wedge \neg A_k \wedge B_{ij} \wedge \neg C_{ij} \wedge \neg C_{jk} \wedge \neg C_{ki}$$
$$\vee \neg A_i \wedge \neg A_j \wedge \neg A_k \wedge B_{ij} \wedge C_{ij} \wedge \neg C_{ki}$$
$$\vee \neg A_i \wedge \neg A_j \wedge \neg A_k \wedge B_{jk} \wedge C_{jk} \wedge \neg C_{ij}$$
$$\vee \neg A_i \wedge \neg A_j \wedge \neg A_k \wedge B_{ki} \wedge C_{ki} \wedge \neg C_{ij}$$
$$\equiv A_i \vee A_j \vee A_k \vee B_{ij} \vee B_{jk} \vee B_{ki}$$

For the subprogram that computes flag $:= 3$ we have

$$\neg A_i \wedge \neg A_j \wedge \neg A_k \wedge C_{ij} \wedge C_{jk} \wedge C_{ki}$$
$$\equiv \neg(A_i \vee A_j \vee A_k \vee B_{ij} \vee B_{jk} \vee B_{ki}) \wedge (C_{ij} \wedge C_{jk} \wedge C_{ki})$$

For the subprogram that computes flag $:= 2$ we have

$$\neg A_i \wedge \neg A_j \wedge \neg A_k \wedge \neg B_{ij} \wedge C_{ij} \wedge \neg C_{ki}$$
$$\vee \neg A_i \wedge \neg A_j \wedge \neg A_k \wedge \neg B_{jk} \wedge C_{jk} \wedge \neg C_{ij}$$
$$\vee \neg A_i \wedge \neg A_j \wedge \neg A_k \wedge \neg B_{ki} \wedge C_{ki} \wedge \neg C_{ij}$$
$$\equiv \neg(A_i \vee A_j \vee A_k \vee B_{ij} \vee B_{jk} \vee B_{ki}) \wedge \neg(C_{ij} \wedge C_{jk} \wedge C_{ki}) \wedge (C_{ij} \vee C_{jk} \vee C_{ki})$$

For the subprogram that computes flag $:= 1$ we have

$$\neg A_i \wedge \neg A_j \wedge \neg A_k \wedge \neg B_{ij} \wedge \neg B_{jk} \wedge \neg B_{ki} \wedge \neg C_{ij} \wedge \neg C_{jk} \wedge \neg C_{ki}$$
$$\equiv \neg(A_i \vee A_j \vee A_k \vee B_{ij} \vee B_{jk} \vee B_{ki}) \wedge \neg(C_{ij} \wedge C_{jk} \wedge C_{ki}) \wedge \neg(C_{ij} \vee C_{jk} \vee C_{ki})$$

Thus, in accordance with Corollary 7.2, Program 5.6 can be rewritten in the following form:

if $A_i \vee A_j \vee A_k \vee B_{ij} \vee B_{jk} \vee B_{ki}$ **then** flag $:= 4$
else if $C_{ij} \wedge C_{jk} \wedge C_{ki}$ **then** flag $:= 3$
else if $C_{ij} \vee C_{jk} \vee C_{ki}$ **then** flag $:= 2$
else flag $:= 1$;

That is, we can refine Program 5.6 by having it decomposed pathwise into a set of subprograms, having each subprogram simplified, and then using the subprograms to recompose the program, which is a significant refinement of the original program. The result is the much simpler following program.

Program 7.3

```
int i, j, k, flag;
read(i, j, k);
if (i ≤ 0 ∨ j ≤ 0 ∨ k ≤ 0 ∨ i+j ≤ k ∨ j+k ≤ i ∨ k+i ≤ j) flag := 4
        else if (i = j ∧ j = k ∧ k = i) flag := 3
        else if (i = j ∨ j = k ∨ k = i) flag := 2
        else flag := 1;
write(flag);
```

Recomposition of a loop construct is more involved. Before setting out to pursue this problem, we need to be able to answer a more fundamental question first. That is, how can we tell if we have used all necessary subprograms in recomposing a given program?

How can a loop construct be recomposed from a finite number of its trace subprograms? The reason is very simple. Consider a loop construct of the form **repeat** S **until** ¬B, whose trace subprograms are formed by a concatenation of the trace subprograms of S. If S is loop free then it is composed of a finite number of trace subprograms. Therefore all information needed to recompose S, and hence **repeat** S **until** ¬B, can be found in a finite subset of trace subprograms of the loop. If S contains loop constructs, the preceding argument can be recursively applied to the inner loops. In the following text theorems that are needed for recomposing a loop construct from its subprograms are developed.

First the following theorem is obvious.

Theorem 7.4

    a. If **while** B **do** S $\Rightarrow$ / \B;S$_1$;/ \B;S$_2$;/ \B;S$_3$; . . . ;/ \B;S$_n$;/ \¬B then **while** B **do** $\{S_1, S_2, \ldots, S_n\} \Rightarrow$ / \B;S$_1$;/ \B;S$_2$;/ \B; . . . ;S$_{n-1}$;/ \B; S$_n$;/ \¬B, and **while** B **do** S $\Rightarrow$ **while** B **do** $\{S_1, S_2, S_3, \ldots, S_n\}$.

    b. If **repeat** S **until** ¬B $\Rightarrow$ S$_1$;/ \B;S$_2$;/ \B;S$_3$; . . . ;/ \B;S$_n$;/ \¬B then **repeat** $\{S_1, S_2, \ldots, S_n\}$ **until** ¬B $\Rightarrow$ S$_1$;/ \B;S$_2$;/ \B; . . . ;S$_{n-1}$;/ \B; S$_n$;/ \¬B, and **repeat** S **until** ¬B $\Rightarrow$ **repeat** $\{S_1, S_2, S_3, \ldots, S_n\}$ **until** ¬B.

Proof. Part a can be proved as now outlined.

    1. If **while** B **do** S $\Rightarrow$ / \B;S$_1$;/ \B;S$_2$;/ \B;S$_3$; . . . ;/ \B;S$_n$;/ \¬B then S $\Rightarrow$ S$_i$ for all $1 \leq i \leq n$ because each S$_i$ must be a trace subprogram of S.

    2. Because S $\Rightarrow$ S$_i$ and S $\Rightarrow$ S$_j$ implies S $\Rightarrow$ $\{S_i, S_j\}$, it follows that S $\Rightarrow$ $\{S_1, S_2, \ldots, S_n\}$.

    3. S $\Rightarrow$ S$'$ implies that **while** B **do** S $\Rightarrow$ **while** B **do** S$'$.

                                                             End of Proof

How do we know then, if we have all nonredundant subprograms of S in $\{S_1, S_2, \ldots S_n\}$ such that **while** B **do** $\{S_1, S_2, \ldots S_n\} \Leftrightarrow$ **while** B **do** S? Or **repeat** $\{S_1, S_2, \ldots S_n\}$ **until** ¬B $\Leftrightarrow$ **repeat** S **until** ¬B? We now set out to answer this question in the following corollary.

Corollary 7.5

For programs S, S$_1$, and S$_2$, if S $\Rightarrow$ S$_1$ and S $\Rightarrow$ S$_2$ then S $\Rightarrow$ $\{S_1, S_2\}$.

Proof. By definition, $S \Rightarrow S_1$ and $S \Rightarrow S_2$ implies $(wp(S_1, R) \supset wp(S, R)) \wedge (wp(S_2, R) \supset wp(S, R))$, which is logically equivalent to $(wp(S_1, R) \vee wp(S_2, R)) \supset wp(S, R)$, and hence, by definition, $S \Rightarrow \{S_1, S_2\}$.

End of Proof

Next, note that $wp(S, R)$ denotes the precondition under which an execution of S will terminate in a final state satisfying postcondition R, whereas $wp(S, \neg R)$ denotes the precondition under which an execution of S will terminate in a final state not satisfying postcondition R. As explained in Yeh (1977), because $wp(S, R) \vee wp(S, \neg R) \equiv wp(S, R \vee \neg R) \equiv wp(S, T)$, we have the following corollary.

Corollary 7.6

The precondition under which an execution of S will terminate is $wp(S, T)$.

Corollary 7.7

If program S is deterministic then $wp(S, R) \wedge wp(S, \neg R) \equiv F$ for any predicate R.

Proof. If S is deterministic, S cannot produce two different outputs in response to any particular input. Hence the output will always satisfy either R or $\neg R$, but not both. Hence $wp(S, R) \wedge wp(S, \neg R) \equiv F$.

End of Proof

Corollary 7.8

Let S and S' be two programs. If S is deterministic, $S \Rightarrow S'$, and $wp(S, T) \equiv wp(S', T)$, then $S \Leftrightarrow S'$.

Proof.

Let A_1: $wp(S, R) \wedge wp(S, \neg R) \equiv F$, i.e., S is deterministic,

A_2: $(wp(S', R) \supset wp(S, R)) \wedge (wp(S', \neg R) \supset wp(S, \neg R))$, i.e., $S \Rightarrow S'$,

A_3: $wp(S, R) \vee wp(S, \neg R) \equiv wp(S', R) \vee wp(S', \neg R)$, i.e., $wp(S, T) \equiv wp(S', T)$, and

C: $wp(S, R) \equiv wp(S', R)$, or equivalently, $S \Leftrightarrow S'$.

Path-Oriented Program Analysis

The task at hand is to show that $A_1 \wedge A_2 \wedge A_3 \supset C$ is a theorem. We accomplish this by showing that, if C is false, it is impossible to make all A_i's true. (*Note*: Henceforth we shall use $X \leftarrow V$ to denote that X is given the truth value V.)

1. One way to let $C \leftarrow F$ is to let $wp(S, R) \leftarrow F$ and $wp(S', R) \leftarrow T$.
2. But item 1 entails $A_2 \leftarrow F$. That is, A_i's cannot be all true in this case.
3. The only other way to let $C \leftarrow F$ is to let $wp(S, R) \leftarrow T$ and $wp(S', R) \leftarrow F$.
4. Because of item 3, $A_1 \leftarrow T$ if and only if $wp(S, \neg R) \leftarrow F$.
5. Because of items 3 and 4, $A_3 \leftarrow T$ if and only if $wp(S', \neg R) \leftarrow T$.
6. But items 4 and 5 entail $A_2 \leftarrow F$. That is, A_i's cannot be all true if C is false.

Hence $A_1 \wedge A_2 \wedge A_3 \supset C$ is a theorem. *End of Proof*

Corollary 7.9

If $S \Rightarrow S'$ then $/ \setminus C;S \Rightarrow / \setminus C;S'$ for any constraint C.
Proof. $S \Rightarrow S'$ entails $wp(S', R) \supset wp(S, R)$. But

$$wp(S', R) \supset wp(S, R)$$
$$C \wedge wp(S', R) \supset C \wedge wp(S, R)$$
$$wp(/ \setminus C;S', R) \supset wp(/ \setminus C;S. R)$$

which in turn implies that $/ \setminus C;S \Rightarrow / \setminus C;S'$. *End of Proof*

Corollary 7.10

a. If $/ \setminus B;S_1;/ \setminus B;S_2;/ \setminus B;S_3; \ldots;/ \setminus B;S_n;/ \setminus \neg B$ is a trace subprogram of **while** B **do** S then each S_i $(1 \le i \le n)$ is a trace subprogram of S.
b. If $S_1;/ \setminus B;S_2;/ \setminus B;S_3; \ldots;/ \setminus B;S_n;/ \setminus \neg B$ is a trace subprogram of **repeat** S **until** $\neg B$, then each S_i $(1 \le i \le n)$ is a trace subprogram of S.

Proof. It immediately follows from the semantics of a **repeat** construct and Definition 5.1a.

Theorem 7.11

Let S and S′ be two programs.

    a. If (1) S is deterministic, (2) Q is a loop invariant of $/\backslash Q$; **while** B **do** S, (3) S $\Rightarrow$ S′, and (4) wp($/\backslash Q$;S, T) $\equiv$ wp($/\backslash Q$;S′, T), then Q is also a loop invariant of $/\backslash Q$; **while** B **do** S′.

    b. If (1) S is deterministic, (2) Q is a loop invariant of $/\backslash Q$; **repeat** S **until** ¬B, (3) S $\Rightarrow$ S′, and (4) wp($/\backslash Q$;S, T) $\equiv$ wp($/\backslash Q$;S′, T), then Q is also a loop invariant of $/\backslash Q$; **repeat** S′ **until** ¬B.

Proof. What follows is a proof of Part a. Part b can be similarly proved. Let

A_1:   wp(S, Q) $\wedge$ wp(S, ¬Q) $\equiv$ F, i.e., S is deterministic,

A_2:   Q $\wedge$ B $\supset$ wp(S, Q), i.e., Q is a loop invariant of $/\backslash Q$; **while** B **do** S,

A_3:   (wp(S′, Q) $\supset$ wp(S, Q)) $\wedge$ (wp(S′, ¬Q) $\supset$ wp(S, ¬Q)), i.e., S $\Rightarrow$ S′,

A_4:   wp($/\backslash Q$;S, T) $\equiv$ wp($/\backslash Q$;S′, T), which is logically equivalent to Q $\wedge$ (wp(S, Q) $\vee$ wp(S, ¬Q)) $\equiv$ Q $\wedge$ (wp(S′, Q) $\vee$ wp(S′, ¬Q)), and

C: Q $\wedge$ B $\supset$ wp(S′, Q), i.e., Q is a loop invariant of $/\backslash Q$; **while** B **do** S′.

The task at hand is to show that $A_1 \wedge A_2 \wedge A_3 \wedge A_4 \supset$ C is a theorem. We accomplish this by showing that, if C is false, it is impossible to make all A_i's true.

    1. Let C be false. This is possible if and only if Q $\leftarrow$ T, B $\leftarrow$ T and wp(S′, Q) $\leftarrow$ F.

    2. Because of item 1, $A_2 \leftarrow$ T if and only if wp(S, Q) $\leftarrow$ T.

    3. Because of items 1 and 2, $A_4 \leftarrow$ T if and only if wp(S′, ¬Q) $\leftarrow$ T.

    4. Because of items 1 and 3, $A_3 \leftarrow$ T if and only if wp(S, ¬Q) $\leftarrow$ T.

    5. But items 2 and 4 entail $A_1 \leftarrow$ F. That is, A_i's cannot be all true if C is false.

Hence $A_1 \wedge A_2 \wedge A_3 \wedge A_4 \supset$ C is a theorem.   *End of Proof*

Theorem 7.12

If S $\Leftrightarrow$ S′ then

a. while B do S $\Leftrightarrow$ while B do S$'$.
b. repeat S until $\neg$B $\Leftrightarrow$ repeat S$'$ until $\neg$B.

Proof. The proof of part a only is given. Part b follows immediately because **repeat** S **until** $\neg$B $\Leftrightarrow$ S; **while** B **do** S.
By definition (Yeh, 1977),

wp(**while** B **do** S, R)
$\equiv (\exists j)_{j \geq 0}(A_j(S, R))$,

where $A_0(S, R) \equiv \neg B \wedge R$ and $A_{j+1}(S, R) \equiv B \wedge wp(S, A_j(S, R))$, $A_0(S', R) \equiv \neg B \wedge R$, and $A_{j+1}(S', R) \equiv B \wedge wp(S', A_j(S', R))$).
It suffices to show that $A_j(S, R) \equiv A_j(S', R)$ for all $j \geq 0$. Obviously, $A_j(S, R) \equiv A_j(S', R)$ is true for $j = 0$. Now, assume that it is true for some $j = n$, i.e., $A_n(S, R) \equiv A_n(S', R)$. Because $S \Leftrightarrow S'$, wp(S, R) $\equiv$ wp(S$'$, R) for any postcondition R, it follows that wp(S, $A_n(S, R)$) $\equiv$ wp(S$'$, $A_n(S', R)$) and thus $A_{n+1}(S, R) \equiv A_{n+1}(S', R)$. Thus, by the principle of mathematical induction, $A_j(S, R) \equiv A_j(S', R)$ for all $j \geq 0$. *End of Proof*

Theorem 7.13

a. If Q is a loop invariant of **while** B **do** S then
/ \Q; **while** B **do** S $\Leftrightarrow$ / \Q; **while** B **do** / \Q;S.
b. If Q is a loop invariant of **repeat** S **until** $\neg$B then
/ \Q; **repeat** S **until** $\neg$B $\Leftrightarrow$ / \Q; **repeat** / \Q;S **until** $\neg$B.

Proof. The proof of Part b only is given. Part a can be proved in the same manner.
Observe that the trace subprogram that iterates the loop body S in / \Q; **repeat** S **until** $\neg$B is

TRACE1: / \Q; S; / \B; S; / \B; S; ... ; / \B; S; / \$\neg$B,

and that iterates the loop body / \Q;S in / \Q;**repeat** / \Q;S **until** $\neg$B for exactly the same number of times is

TRACE2: / \Q; S; / \B; / \Q; S; / \B; / \Q; S; ... ; / \B; / \Q; S; / \$\neg$B.

The latter is logically equivalent to the former because, if Q is a loop invariant of **repeat** S **until** ¬B, then Q ⊃ wp(S, Q), and therefore Q ∧ wp(S, Q) ≡ Q. This allows us to establish the following relationship:

$$/\setminus Q;\ S;\ /\setminus B;\ /\setminus Q;\ S \quad \Leftrightarrow\ /\setminus Q;\ S;\ /\setminus B;\ /\setminus Q;\ S$$
$$\Leftrightarrow\ /\setminus Q;\ S;\ /\setminus Q;\ /\setminus B;\ S$$
$$\Leftrightarrow\ /\setminus Q;\ /\setminus wp(S,\ Q);\ S;\ /\setminus B;\ S$$
$$\Leftrightarrow\ /\setminus Q \wedge wp(S,\ Q);\ S;\ /\setminus B;\ S$$
$$\Leftrightarrow\ /\setminus Q;\ S;\ /\setminus B;\ S,$$

which can be repeatedly applied to TRACE2, from right to left, to eliminate every constraint $/\setminus Q$, except the first. The resulting trace subprogram is identical to TRACE1. Hence the proof.   *End of Proof*

The following three theorems represent the main results of the work on recomposition of a loop construct from its trace subprograms. Although they are stated in terms of "**repeat** S **until** ¬B" constructs, they are directly applicable to "**while** B **do** S" constructs as well.

The first of these theorems sets out the conditions under which the loop body of a loop may be replaced with a set of its subprograms.

Theorem 7.14

For a loop construct of the form **repeat** S **until** ¬B, if

1. $S, S_1, S_2, \ldots, S_n$ are deterministic programs such that $S \Rightarrow S_i$ for all $1 \le i \le n$,
2. Q is a loop invariant of **repeat** S **until** ¬B, and
3. $wp(/\setminus Q;S,\ T) \equiv wp(/\setminus Q;\{S_1, S_2, \ldots, S_n\},\ T)$, then $/\setminus Q;$**repeat** S **until** ¬B $\Leftrightarrow /\setminus Q;$**repeat** $\{S_1, S_2, \ldots, S_n\}$ **until** ¬B.

Proof. Because of Parts 1 and 2, and by Corollary 7.5, $S \Rightarrow \{S_1, S_2, \ldots, S_n\}$.

By Corollary 7.9, $/\setminus Q;\ S \Rightarrow /\setminus Q;\ \{S_1, S_2, \ldots, S_n\}$. In accordance with Theorem 7.8, this relation, together with Part 3, entails $/\setminus Q;\ S \Leftrightarrow /\setminus Q;\ \{S_1, S_2, \ldots, S_n\}$.

By Theorem 7.11, Q is also a loop invariant of **repeat** $\{S_1, S_2, \ldots, S_n\}$ **until** ¬B as well.

Hence, by Corollaries 7.9 and 7.10,

$$/ \backslash Q; \textbf{repeat } S \textbf{ until } \neg B$$
$$\Leftrightarrow \quad / \backslash Q; \textbf{repeat } / \backslash Q; S \textbf{ until } \neg B$$
$$\Leftrightarrow \quad / \backslash Q; \textbf{repeat } / \backslash Q; \{S_1, S_2, \ldots, S_n\} \textbf{ until } \neg B.$$
$$\Leftrightarrow \quad / \backslash Q; \textbf{repeat } \{S_1, S_2, \ldots, S_n\} \textbf{ until } \neg B. \qquad \textit{End of Proof}$$

There are two special cases in which Part 3 of Theorem 7.14 becomes satisfied. The first is when $wp(\{S_1, S_2, \ldots, S_n\}, T) \equiv T$. In that case, because of Part 1 and Corollary 7.5, $S \Rightarrow \{S_1, S_2, \ldots, S_n\}$. By Definition 2.5, $wp(\{S_1, S_2, \ldots, S_n\}, R) \supset wp(S, R)$ for any R. Since $wp(\{S_1, S_2, \ldots, S_n\}, T) \equiv T$ it follows that $wp(S, T) \equiv T$. Thus, by Theorems 7.8 and 7.12, we have

Theorem 7.15

For a loop construct of the form **repeat** S **until** $\neg B$, if

1. $S, S_1, S_2, \ldots, S_n$ are deterministic programs such that $S \Rightarrow S_i$ for all $1 \leq i \leq n$, and
2. $wp(\{S_1, S_2, \ldots, S_n\}, T) \equiv T$,

then **repeat** S **until** $\neg B \Leftrightarrow$ **repeat** $\{S_1, S_2, \ldots, S_n\}$ **until** $\neg B$.

The second special case is that $wp(\{S_1, S_2, \ldots, S_n\}, T)$ is a loop invariant of **repeat** $\{S_1, S_2, \ldots, S_n\}$ **until** $\neg B$. In that case, Theorem 7.14 can be restated as follows.

Theorem 7.16

For a loop construct of the form **repeat** S **until** $\neg B$, if

1. $S, S_1, S_2, \ldots, S_n$ are deterministic programs such that $S \Rightarrow S_i$ for all $1 \leq i \leq n$,
2. Q is a loop invariant of **repeat** $\{S_1, S_2, \ldots, S_n\}$ **until** $\neg B$, and
3. $wp(\{S_1, S_2, \ldots, S_n\}, T) \subset Q$,

then $/ \backslash Q$; **repeat** S **until** $\neg B \Leftrightarrow / \backslash Q$; **repeat** $\{S_1, S_2, \ldots, S_n\}$ **until** $\neg B$.

Proof. Assume that there is another subprogram S_{n+1} such that $S \Rightarrow S_{n+1}$ and S_{n+1} is not logically equivalent to S_i for all $1 \leq i \leq n$. Because of Part 1, $wp(S_{n+1}, T) \supset \neg wp(\{S_1, S_2, \ldots, S_n\}, T)$. That means before every iteration of the loop body, Q is true, $wp(\{S_1, S_2, \ldots, S_n\}, T)$ is true, $\neg wp(\{S_1, S_2, \ldots, S_n\}, T)$ is false, and therefore $wp(S_{n+1}, T)$ is false. Hence S_{n+1} will never be selected in any iteration of the loop body, and thus need not be included in the loop body.   *End of Proof*

To demonstrate the utilities of these results, consider the following trace subprogram produced by having Program A.2 instrumented for symbolic trace generation, and then executing the instrumented program with input x = 97.

Program 7.17

```
cin >> x;
y = 1;
/\ x <= 100;
x = x + 11;
y = y + 1;
/\!(x <= 100);
/\ y != 1;
x = x - 10;
y = y - 1;
/\ x <= 100;
x = x + 11;
y = y + 1;
/\!(x <= 100);
/\ y != 1;
x = x - 10;
y = y - 1;
/\ x <= 100;
x = x + 11;
y = y + 1;
/\!(x <= 100);
/\ y != 1;
x = x - 10;
y = y - 1;
/\ x <= 100
x = x + 11;
y = y + 1;
```

Path-Oriented Program Analysis

```
/\!(x <= 100);
/\ y != 1;
x = x - 10;
y = y - 1;
/\!(x <= 100);
/\!(y != 1);
z = x - 10;
cout << "z = " << z;;
```

Note that

```
while (x <= 100) {
    x = x + 11;
    y = y + 1;
}
```
⇒ /\ x <= 100;
```
x = x + 11;
y = y + 1;
/\!(x <= 100);
```

and

```
while (y != 1)
{{{
    x = x - 10;
    y = y - 1;
    /\ x <= 100;
    x = x + 11;
    y = y + 1;
    /\!(x <= 100);
...
    x = x - 10;
    y = y - 1;
    /\!(x <= 100);
}}}
```
⇒
```
/\ y != 1;
    x = x - 10;
    y = y - 1;
    /\ x <= 100;
```

```
x = x + 11;
y = y + 1;
/\!(x <= 100);
/\ y != 1;
x = x - 10;
y = y - 1;
/\ x <= 100;
x = x + 11;
y = y + 1;
/\!(x <= 100);
/\ y != 1;
x = x - 10;
y = y - 1;
/\ x <= 100
x = x + 11;
y = y + 1;
/\!(x <= 100);
/\ y != 1;
x = x - 10;
y = y - 1;
/\!(x <= 100);
/\!(y != 1);
```

Thus, in view of Theorem 7.4, we can write
Program 7.17 $\Rightarrow$

```
cin >> x;
y = 1;
/\ x <= 100;
while (x <= 100) {
        x = x + 11;
        y = y + 1;
}
while (y != 1)
        {{{
            x = x - 10;
            y = y - 1;
            /\ x <= 100;
            x = x + 11;
```

```
          y = y + 1;
          /\!(x <= 100);
      ...
          x = x - 10;
          y = y - 1;
          /\!(x <= 100);
      }}}
z = x - 10;
cout << "z = " << z;;
```

which can be simplified as in Program 7.18.

⇔Program 7.18

```
cin >> x;
y = 1;
/\ x <= 100;
while (x <= 100) {
        x = x + 11;
        y = y + 1;
}
while (y != 1)
        {{{
            /\ x > 99;
            /\ x <= 110;
            x = x + 1;

        ...
            /\ x > 110;
            x = x - 10;
            y = y - 1;
        }}}
z = x - 10;
cout << "z = " << z;
```

It is observed that, in the preceding second loop, there is no trace subprogram designed for the case $x <= 99$. In general, when S, a program, is decomposed into a set of subprograms $\{/\backslash C_1;S_1, /\backslash C_2;S_2, \ldots, /\backslash C_n;S_n\}$, it should have the property that $C_1 \vee C_2 \vee \ldots \vee C_n \equiv T$. It appears that we might have to find other trace subprograms to cover the case x <= 99 in order for Program 7.18 to be logically equivalent to Program A.2.1.

To see if that is indeed the case, let us find the loop invariant of the second loop in Program 7.18. It is relatively easy to find that

```
⇔    cin >> x;
     y = 1;
     /\ x <= 100;
     while (x <= 100) {
          x = x + 11;
          y = y + 1;
     }
     /\ x > 100;
     while (y != 1)
          {{{
               /\ x > 99;
               /\ x <= 110;
               x = x + 1;
               /\ x > 100;

          , , ,
               /\ x > 110;
               x = x - 10;
               y = y - 1;
               /\ x > 100;
          }}}
     z = x - 10;
     cout << "z = " << z;
```

That is, x < 100 is a loop invariant of the second loop in Program 7.18. That being the case, the trace subprograms designed for x <= 99, whatever that may be, will never be executed and thus will not be needed in the second loop.

That is exactly what Theorem 7.16 says in a more formal way: The loop body S has two trace subprograms as subsequently listed:

S_1: /\ x > 99;
     /\ x <= 110;
     x = x + 1;

85

$S_2:$ $/\backslash x > 110;$
 $x = x - 10;$
 $y = y - 1;$

We see that S, S_1, and S_2, are deterministic, and $S \Rightarrow \{S_1, S_2\}$. We also see that $x > 100$ is a loop invariant of **while** B **do** $\{S_1, S_2\}$, and wp($\{S_1, S_2\}$, T) $\equiv x > 99 \land x \leq 110 \lor x > 110 \equiv x > 99$, which is implied by the loop invariant $x > 100$. Therefore, by Theorem 7.16, **while** B **do** S in the first subprogram of Program A.2.1 is equivalent to Program 7.18.

To summarize, we have shown that we can recompose a loop construct from a subset of its trace subprograms.

8

Discussion

The notion of a state constraint introduced in this work led to the development of a formal system useful for several purposes. First and foremost, it allows us to speak formally of the subprogram involved in a particular program execution. The subprogram can be generated automatically by means of program instrumentation (Huang, 1980b). Furthermore, the subprogram can be simplified by use of the rules developed in this work. From the subprogram text we can determine the computation performed as well as the input domain for which it is defined.

This has an important application in program testing. It is well known that there is very little we can conclude from a successful test execution: If a program produces a correct result for a test case, then all we can say is that that program is correct with respect to that test case. By using the result presented in this work, however, we can automatically generate the subprogram involved, and from that subprogram we can determine the exact nature of computation performed during the test, as well as the domain for which that subprogram is defined.

To illustrate, let us consider Program A.2.1 in Appendix A again.

Path-Oriented Program Analysis

Program A.2.1

```
cin >> x;
y = 1;
/\ x <= 100;
while (x <= 100) {
    x = x + 11;
    y = y + 1;
}
while (y != 1) {
    x = x - 10;
    y = y - 1;
    while (x <= 100) {
        x = x + 11;
        y = y + 1;
    }
}
z = x - 10;
cout << "z = " << z << endl;
```

In accordance with the discussion given in Chapter 5, this program can be represented by the program graph shown in the figure,

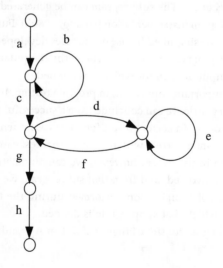

where, for clarity, the program component associated with each edge is
denoted by a symbol as follows:

```
a:  cin >> x;
    y = 1;
b:  /\x <= 100;
    x = x + 11;
    y = y + 1;
c:  /\x > 100;
d:  /\ y != 1;
    x = x - 10;
    y = y - 1;
e:  /\x <= 100;
    x = x + 11;
    y = y + 1
f:  /\x > 100;
g:  /\y == 1;
h:  z = x - 10;
    cout << "z = " << z << endl;
```

Recall that this program is designed to compute the following function:
if $x = 100$ then $z = 91$ else $z = x - 10$. Now suppose this program
was test-executed with $x = 123$ and the program printed "$z = 113$" as
the result. All we can conclude from this test result is that the program
works correctly for the input $x = 123$.

It is easy to see that, for $x = 123$, the program will execute along the
path *acgh*. Therefore, the subprogram involved in this test is

```
acgh:   cin >> x;
        y = 1;
        /\x > 100;
        /\y == 1;
        z = x - 10;
        cout << "z = " << z << endl;
```

which can be readily simplified to

```
⇔   cin >> x;
    /\ x > 100;
```

Path-Oriented Program Analysis

```
z = x - 10;
cout << "z = " << z << endl;
```

We can readily see that the "else" part of the specification is correctly implemented by this subprogram.

Note that the preceding subprogram (associated with execution path *acgh*) is defined not only for x = 123 but also for any x > 100. Hence it is useful to obtain and to analyze that subprogram because it tells us not only what the program will do for x = 123 but also for many others as well.

Those who are familiar with the concept of symbolic execution (King, 1975) will note that we can obtain the same result by symbolically executing the program along the path *acgh* to yield z = X − 10, with the path condition X > 100 (X being the symbolic value of the input). That is, symbolic execution is equally useful in this instance, viz., for analyzing an execution path defined for multiple inputs.

It must be noted, however, that many execution paths are defined just for one input. For instance, if we execute Program A.2.1 with x = 97, the subprogram involved is Program 7.17, which can be simplified to the following one:

```
cin >> x;
/\ x == 97;
z = 91;
cout << "z = " << z << endl;
```

This simplified subprogram shows that it is defined for only one input, viz., x = 97, and it does nothing but assign 91 to output variable z.

Again, the technique of symbolic execution can be used to reach the same conclusion. However, the fact that, for input x = 97, the program will assign 91 to z can be much more readily ascertained by a test-execution instead!

In general, if the program contains a loop, and if the loop can be iterated for a great many number of times, the program can also be decomposed into as many trace subprograms. A subprogram formed by a particular iteration of the loop is often defined for only one element in the input domain. In that case, the technique of symbolic execution cannot be used to add any information to what is already known through a test-execution.

Definition 8.1

A subprogram (or a program execution path) is said to be *singular* if it is defined for one, and only one, input.

Unlike symbolic execution, which is developed to deal with one execution path at a time, the present method can be used to analyze a subprogram that includes multiple execution paths or loop constructs. Thus, if we found that the subprogram to be analyzed is singular, we can first expand its domain of definition by combining it with other subprograms or recompose the loop constructs involved as described in Chapter 7.

For example, suppose we are given Program 7.17, which is singularly defined for input x = 97. If we recompose the loop constructs involved, the result is Program 7.18, which is a subprogram defined for all x ≤ 100. The present method can then be applied to simplify it to determine what Program A.2.1 does for x ≤ 100, as subsequently shown.

Program 7.18

```
cin >> x;
y = 1;
/\ x <= 100;
while (x <= 100) {
    x = x + 11;
    y = y + 1;
}
while (y != 1)
    {{{
        /\ x > 99
        /\ x <= 110;
        x = x + 1;
    ,,,
        /\ x > 110;
        x = x - 10;
        y = y - 1;
    }}}
z = x - 10;
cout << "z = " << z << endl;
```

```
⇔   cin >> x;
    /\ x <= 100;
    z = 91;
    cout << "z = " << z << endl;
```

The preceding subprogram clearly shows that, for any input $x \leq 100$, Program A.2.1 does nothing but assign 91 to z. This result cannot be produced through testing or symbolic execution.

Another major achievement of this work is that it provides a unified framework for both program testing as well as proving program correctness. To show that a program S is (partially) correct with respect to input predicate I and output predicate R (i.e., I{S}R in Hoare's formalism) is to show that constraint R in program / \I;S;/ \R is tautological, as shown in Chapter 6.

Most corollaries and theorems in this work can be interpreted as program verification rules, some of which are restatements of known verification rules in terms of the new formalism. For instance, Theorems 6.7, Part a, and 6.8, Part a, are a variation of the invariant relation theorem (Dijkstra, 1976). Theorem 6.5 is new. Although it does not make the correctness of a loop construct easier to prove, it often suggests possible candidates for the loop invariants and provides a different, and possibly a more intuitive, view of what needs to be done in constructing the proof.

The new formalism developed in this book also makes it easier for us to tackle the question of whether or not a loop construct can be reconstructed from its trace. The last, but not least, major accomplishment of this work is an answer to this question stated as Theorem 7.16.

The graphic program representation scheme introduced in Chapter 5 also provides an efficient mechanism for proving the equivalence of certain programming constructs. For instance, it is known that

> while B do S ⇔ while B ∧ wp(S, B) do begin S;S end;
> while B do S.

This is the formal basis for speeding up execution of a "while" loop through generalized loop unrolling (Huang and Leng, 1999; Leng, 2001). The relation just stated says that we can prefix a **while B do** S statement with the following loop construct, while B ∧ wp(S, B) **do begin** S; S **end**,

without changing the computation it performs. This new "while" statement will check to see if B will be true in the next two iterations, and, if
so, it will proceed to execute S twice. Otherwise, the loop will terminate
and the execution will proceed to the original "while" statement that
follows. The execution will either terminate if B becomes false at that
juncture or will proceed to iterate the loop once if B is true. Now, if we
can somehow simplify the computation required for evaluating predicate wp(S, B) or the computation prescribed by S;S, we will be able to
speed up the computation because this new loop will iterate only half
as many times as the original. The original loop that follows will iterate
only once, or not at all.

The validity of this equivalence relation is intuitively clear. But how
do we prove it formally? It turns out that we can construct a very succinct
proof by using the graphic program representation scheme described in
Chapter 5. The program graphs of constructs on both sides of the "⇔"
symbol are depicted in the figure.

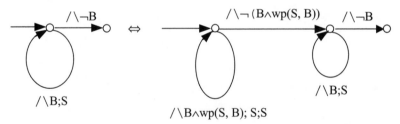

Because we can describe the execution paths from entry to exit of
these two program graphs by using regular expressions, all we need to
do, therefore, is to show that

$$(/\backslash B;S)^*;(/\backslash \neg B) \Leftrightarrow (/\backslash B;S;/\backslash B;S)^*;/\backslash \neg(B \land wp(S, B));(/\backslash B;S)^*;(/\backslash \neg B)$$

This can be done as follows:

$$(/\backslash B;S;/\backslash B;S)^*;/\backslash \neg(B \land wp(S, B));(/\backslash B;S)^*;(/\backslash \neg B)$$
$$\Leftrightarrow (/\backslash B;S;/\backslash B;S)^*;/\backslash \neg B \lor \neg wp(S, B);(/\backslash B;S)^*(/\backslash \neg B)$$
$$\Leftrightarrow (/\backslash B;S;/\backslash B;S)^*;\{/\backslash \neg B;(/\backslash B;S)^*, /\backslash \neg wp(S, B);(/\backslash B;S)^*\};/\backslash \neg B$$
$$\Leftrightarrow (/\backslash B;S;/\backslash B;S)^*;\{\lambda, /\backslash B;S\};/\backslash \neg B$$
$$\Leftrightarrow (/\backslash B;S)^*;/\backslash \neg B$$

Hence the proof.

In deriving the preceding equality, we made use of the following relations:

$$/ \setminus \neg B; (/ \setminus B; S)^* \Leftrightarrow \lambda$$
$$/ \setminus \neg wp(S, B); (/ \setminus B; S)^* \Leftrightarrow / \setminus B; S$$

It shall be mentioned in passing that a "while" loop can be unrolled more than once because

while B **do** S

$\Leftrightarrow$ **while** B$\wedge$wp(S, B) **do begin** S;S **end; while** B **do** S

$\Leftrightarrow$ **while** B$\wedge$wp(S, B)$\wedge$wp(S, wp(S, B)) **do begin** S;S;S **end; while B do** S

$\Leftrightarrow$ **while** B$\wedge$wp(S, B)$\wedge$wp(S, wp(S, B))$\wedge$wp(S, wp(S, wp(S, B))) **do begin** S;S;S;S **end; while** B **do** S

$\Leftrightarrow$ . . .

and the proof of these relations can be constructed similarly.

Automatic Generation of Symbolic Traces

The symbolic traces or trace subprograms of a program can be generated automatically through static analysis or program instrumentation. By program instrumentation we mean the process in which we insert additional statements into the program for the purpose of collecting information about the program that is useful for anything other than computing the intended function.

To generate symbolic traces through static analysis, we determine the syntax of the program first, construct its program graph as defined in Chapter 5, find all paths of interest, and then represent the paths as regular expressions over the edge symbols. For any path described by regular expression, we can obtain its symbolic trace simply by replacing all edge symbols with the corresponding program components.

For example, consider the following C++ program:

```
int main()
{
    int x, y, z;
    cin >> x >> y;
```

Path-Oriented Program Analysis

```
z = 1;
while (y != 0) {
    if (y % 2 == 1)
        z = z * x;
    y = y / 2;
    x = x * x;
}
    cout << z << endl;
}
```

Subsequently shown is the program graph of this program:

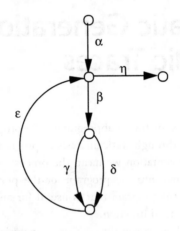

```
where α:  cin >> x >> y ;
          z = 1;
      β:  /\ y != 0;
      γ:  /\!(y % 2 == 1);
      δ:  /\ y % 2 == 1;
          z = z * x;
      ε:  y = y / 2;
          x = x * x;
      η:  /\!(y != 0);
          cout << z << endl;
```

The set of all paths from the entry to the exit can be denoted by a regular expression, such as $\alpha(\beta(\gamma+\delta)\epsilon)^*\eta$. (*Note*: It can be equivalently represented by many other regular expressions.) Now suppose we are interested in the set of two paths, $\{\alpha\beta\delta\epsilon\eta, \alpha\beta\gamma\epsilon\eta\}$, for some reason. We can obtain the symbolic traces of these two paths by replacing the edge symbols with the corresponding program components as subsequently listed:

```
αβδεη:      cin >> x >> y ;
            z = 1;
            /\ y != 0;
            /\ y % 2 == 1;
            z = z * x;
            y = y / 2;
            x = x * x;
            /\!(y != 0);
            cout << z << endl;
αβγεη:      cin >> x >> y ;
            z = 1;
            /\ y != 0;
            /\!(y % 2 == 1);
            y = y / 2;
            x = x * x;
            /\!(y != 0);
            cout << z << endl;
```

It should be relatively straightforward to build a software tool to auto-mate this process. The problem with this method is that it will gen-erate symbolic traces representing feasible as well as infeasible exe-cution paths. Because all programs have many infeasible paths that are of interest to no one, and because it requires a considerable amount of effort to identify such paths, this method of symbolic-trace generation is not suitable for applications in which efficiency matters.

We can overcome this problem by using the technique of program instrumentation. The idea is to insert additional statements into the pro-gram to print out the statement just executed in an appropriate format;

then the symbolic trace will be produced automatically by executing that instrumented program along the path.

The syntax of the host programming language and the format of statements in trace subprograms dictate the way instrumentation is to be done. The format of statements should be chosen to facilitate analysis. For example, a trace subprogram can be expressed as a constrained subprogram as defined in the preceding chapters.

For programs in C++ language, a trace subprogram may be generated as follows. First, we need to define the format in which each statement or predicate is to appear in the trace subprogram. For this purpose, we use "TRACE(S) = t" as the shorthand notation for "statement S is to appear as t in the trace subprogram".

The software instrumentation tool will instrument a program for symbolic-trace generation as follows. For every statement S in the source code to be instrumented, the tool will find TRACE(S), assign a trace number TN(S) to S, store TN(S) as well as TRACE(S) in a file, and then replace S with INST(S) that consists of S as well as the instruments (additional statements designed to generate the trace).

Subsequently listed are the definitions of TRACE(S) followed by those of INST(S) for certain types of statements in C++. The intention of this list is not to provide a complete blueprint for building the required software tool but rather to show how TRACE(S) and INST(S) can be defined for types of statements commonly found in a modern programming language like C++. Therefore, no attempt has been made to list all types of statements exhaustively.

1. Expression statement

> `TRACE(E;) = E` if E is an expression statement.

Examples: The trace subprogram of assignment statement `x = 1` is simply `x = 1` itself, and that of `cin >> first >> character` is `cin >> first >> character` itself.

The syntax of C++ language allows the use of certain shorthand notation in writing an expression statement. To facilitate symbolic analysis, such notation should be rewritten in full in a trace subprogram as exemplified in the table.

statement	trace subprogram
++n;	n = n + 1
-n;	n = n - 1
x = ++n;	n = n + 1
	x = n
x = n++;	x = n
	n = n + 1
i += 2;	i = i + 2
x *= y + 1;	x = x * (y + 1)

2. Conditional Statement:

```
(a) TRACE(if (P) S) = /\ P
                         TRACE(S)        if P is true,
      TRACE(if (P) S) = /\ !(P)         otherwise.
```

P is enclosed in parentheses because it may contain an operator with a priority lower that that of the unary operator "!". Incorrect interpretation of P may result if the parentheses are omitted.

Example: The trace subprogram of statement

```
    if (c ==  '\n') ++n;
```

is dependent on the value of c just before this statement is executed. If it is '\n' (new line) then the trace subprogram is

```
/\ c  ==  '\n'
++n;
```

Otherwise it is

```
/\!(c  ==  '\n')
```

```
(b) TRACE(if (P) S₁ else S₂) = /\ P
                                  TRACE(S₁)    if P is true,
      TRACE(if (P) S₁ else S₂) = /\!(P)
                                  TRACE(S₂)    otherwise.
```

```
(c) TRACE(if (P₁) S₁
            else if (P₂) S₂
```

```
                else if (P₃) S₃
                        .
                        .
                        .
                else if (Pₙ) Sₙ
                else Sₙ₊₁)
        =       /\ !(P₁)
                /\ !(P₂)
                   .
                   .
                   .
                /\ Pᵢ
                TRACE(Sᵢ)                      if Pᵢ is true for some 1 ≤ i ≤ n,
        =       /\ !(P₁)
                /\ !(P₂)
                   .
                   .
                   .
                /\!(Pₙ)
                TRACE(Sₙ₊₁)                    otherwise.
```

3. WHILE statement:

```
    TRACE(while (B) S) = /\ B
                         TRACE(S)
                         /\ B
                         TRACE(S)
                            .
                            .
                            .
                         /\ B
                         TRACE(S)
                         /\!(B)
```

Example: For the following statements,

```
    i = 1;
    while (i <= 3)
    i = i + 1;
```

the trace subprogram is defined to be

```
i = 1;
/\ i <= 3
i = i + 1;
/\ i <= 3
i = i + 1;
/\ i <= 3
i = i + 1;
/\!(i <= 3)
```

4. DO statement:

```
TRACE(do S while (B))  =  TRACE(S)
                          /\ B
                          TRACE(S)
                          /\ B
                              .
                              .
                              .
                          TRACE(S)
                          /\!(B)
```

5. FOR statement:

```
TRACE(for (E₁, E₂, E₃) S)  =  E₁
                              /\ E₂
                              TRACE(S)
                              E₃
                              /\ E₂
                              TRACE(S)
                              E₃
                              .
                              .
                              .
                              /\!(E₂)
```

Example: The trace subprogram of the following statement,

```
for(x = 1; x <= 3; x = x + 1)
    sum = sum + x;
```

is defined to be

```
x  =  1;
/\ x <=  3
sum  =  sum + x;
x  =  x + 1;
/\ x <=  3
sum  =  sum + x;
x  =  x + 1;
/\ x <=  3
sum  =  sum + x;
x  =  x + 1;
/\!(x <=  3)
```

6. SWITCH statement:

```
TRACE(switch (C) {
        case C₁: S₁;
        case C₂: S₂;
                .

                .

                .
        case Cₙ: Sₙ;
        default: Sₙ₊₁;})
```

$= \; /\backslash \; C \; == \; C_i$

$\quad$ TRACE(S_i) if $C = C_i$ for some $1 \leq i \leq n$, assuming that S_i ends

$\qquad\qquad$ with a "break" statement,

$= \; /\backslash \; C \; != \; (C_1)$

$\quad /\backslash \; C \; != \; (C_2)$

$\qquad .$

$\qquad .$

$\qquad .$

$/\backslash \; C \; != \; (C_n)$

TRACE(S_{n+1}) otherwise.

Note: Parentheses around C_i's are needed because C_i's may contain operators such as "&", "∧", and "|", which have a precedence lower than that of " ==" and "!=".

7. BREAK statement:

$$\mathsf{TRACE(break;)} \ = \ \text{empty string}$$
(i.e., need not generate trace subprogram for such a statement)

8. CONTINUE statement:

$$\mathsf{TRACE(continue;)} \ = \ \text{empty string}$$

9. RETURN statement:

(a) $\mathsf{TRACE(return;)} \ = \ \mathsf{return}$
(b) $\mathsf{TRACE(return\ E;)} \ = \ \mathsf{return\ E}$

10. EXIT statement:

(a) $\mathsf{TRACE(exit;)} \ = \ \mathsf{exit}$
(b) $\mathsf{TRACE(exit\ E;)} \ = \ \mathsf{exit\ E}$

11. GOTO statement:

$$\mathsf{TRACE(goto\ LABEL;)} \ = \ \text{empty string}$$

12. Labeled statement:

$$\mathsf{TRACE(LABEL:\ S;)} \ = \ \mathsf{TRACE(S)}$$

13. Null statement:

$$\mathsf{TRACE(;)} \ = \ \text{empty string}$$

14. Compound statement:

$$\mathsf{TRACE(\{\text{declaration-list, statement-list}\})} \ = \ \mathsf{TRACE(\text{statement-list})}$$
$$\mathsf{TRACE(S_1;\ S_2;)} \ = \ \mathsf{TRACE(S_1)}$$
$$\mathsf{TRACE(S_2)}$$

The instrumentation tool examines each statement in the program, constructs its trace as previously defined, assigns an identification number called TN (trace number) to the trace, and stores the trace with its TN in a file. The tool then constructs INST(S), which stands for "the instrumented version of statement S," and writes it into a file created for storing the instrumented version of the program. Production of the trace is done by the program execution monitor pem(). A function call pem(TN(S)) causes the trace of S numbered TN(S) to be fetched from the file and appended to the trace being constructed. The definition of INST(S) is as subsequently given:

1. Expression Statement: If E is an expression, then

INST(E;) = pem (TN(E));
  E;

e.g., if 35 is the trace number associated with statement

cout << "This is a test" << endl;

then

INST(cout << "This is a test" << endl;) = pem (35);
  cout << "This is a test"
  << endl;

2. Condition Statement:

INST(if (P) S) = if (P) {
  pem (TN(P));
  INST(S)
  }
  else
  pem (TN(!(P)));
INST(if (P) S₁ else S₂) = if (P) {
  pem(TN(P));
  INST(S₁)
  }
  else {
  pem (TN(!(P)));
  INST(S₂)
  }

Note that the "if" statement may be nested, i.e., S_1 or S_2 may be another "if" statement. With the instrumentation method described recursively as just shown, we do not need a special rule to deal with nested "if" statements, or to instrument "if" statements of the form (c) given previously.

3. WHILE Statement:

$$
\text{INST(while (P) S)} \quad = \quad
\begin{array}{l}
\text{while (P) \{} \\
\quad \text{pem (TN(P));} \\
\quad \text{INST(S)} \\
\text{\}} \\
\text{pem (TN(!(P)));}
\end{array}
$$

4. DO Statement:

$$
\begin{array}{l}
\text{INST(do S while} \\
\text{(P);)}
\end{array}
\quad = \quad
\begin{array}{l}
\text{\_do\_?:} \\
\\
\text{INST(S)} \\
\text{if (P) \{} \\
\quad \text{pem (TN(P));} \\
\quad \text{goto \_do\_?;} \\
\text{\}} \\
\text{else} \\
\text{pem (TN(!(P)));}
\end{array}
$$

The question mark here will be replaced with an integer assigned by the analyzer-instrumentor. Note that it is incorrect to instrument the DO statement as subsequently shown:

```
do {
INST(S)
if (P) pem (TN(P));
}
while (P);
pem (TN(!(P)));
```

The reason is that predicate P will be evaluated twice here. If P contains a shorthand or an assignment operator, the instrumented program will no longer be computationally equivalent to the original one.

Path-Oriented Program Analysis

5. FOR Statement:

$$\text{INST(for } (E_1; E_2; E_3) \text{ S)} \quad = \quad \begin{array}{l} \text{pem (TN}(E_1)); \\ \text{for } (E_1; E_2; E_3) \, \{ \\ \text{pem (TN}(E_2)); \\ \text{INST(S)} \\ \text{pem (TN}(E_3)); \\ \} \\ \text{pem (TN}(!(E_2))); \end{array}$$

6. SWITCH Statement:

```
INST(switch (C) {
     case C₁: S₁
     case C₂: S₂


     case Cₙ: Sₙ
  default: Sₙ₊₁})
```

$$= \quad \begin{array}{l} \{\text{int } \_i\_; \\ \_i\_ = 0; \\ \text{switch (C) } \{ \\ \text{case } C_1: \text{ if } (\_i\_++ == 0) \text{ pem (TN(C } == (C_1))); \\ \text{INST}(S_1) \\ \text{case } C_2: \text{ if } (\_i\_++ == 0) \text{ pem (TN(C } == (C_2))); \\ \text{INST}(S_2) \\ . \\ . \\ . \\ \text{case } C_n: \text{ if } (\_i\_++ == 0) \text{ pem (TN(C } == (C_n))); \\ \text{INST}(S_n) \\ \text{default: if } (\_i\_++ == 0) \, \{ \\ \text{pem (TN(C! } = (C_1))); \\ \text{pem (TN(C! } = (C_2))); \\ . \\ . \\ . \\ \text{pem (TN(C! } = (C_n))); \\ \} \\ \text{INST}(S_{n+1}) \\ \} \\ \} \end{array}$$

The reason why we use _i_ here is that cases serve just as labels. After the code for one case is done, execution falls through to the next unless we take explicit action to escape. The flag _i_ is used to ensure that only the condition that is true is included in the trace subprogram.

7. RETURN Statement:

$$INST(return;) \quad = \quad pem\ (TN(return));$$
$$return;$$
$$INST(return\ E;) \quad = \quad pem\ (TN(return\ E));$$
$$return\ E;$$

8. EXIT Statement:

$$INST(exit;) \quad = \quad pem\ (TN(exit));$$
$$exit;$$
$$INST(exit\ E;) \quad = \quad pem\ (TN(exit\ E));$$
$$exit\ E;$$

9. Labeled Statement:

$$INST(LABEL:\ S) \quad = \quad LABEL:\ INST(S)$$

10. Compound Statement:

$$INST(\{declaration\text{-}list \quad = \quad \{$$
$$statement\text{-}list\})$$
$$declaration\text{-}list$$
$$INST(statement\text{-}list)$$
$$\}$$
$$INST(S_1;\ S_2) \quad = \quad INST(S_1)$$
$$INST(S_2)$$

11. Other Statements:

$$INST(break;) \quad = \quad break;$$
$$INST(continue;) \quad = \quad continue;$$
$$INST(goto\ LABEL;) \quad = \quad goto\ LABEL;$$
$$INST(;) \quad = \quad ;$$

Appendix A: Examples

Presented in this appendix are four examples showing in various degrees of detail how the present method can be applied to programs written in C++.

Example A.1 shows how to insert constraints into a program to form a subprogram representing an execution path. It also shows how the rules developed in Chapter 3 can be used to simplify the subprogram to the extent possible.

Example A.2 shows that the present method is not only applicable to an execution path but also to the one that includes a loop construct as well. The analysis is done for all possible execution paths in the program, and thus the result constitutes a direct proof of the correctness.

The program in Example A.3 is adopted from a legacy software tool. A portion of this program (printed in boldface type) is difficult to understand. When the present method was used to analyze that part of the program, it was found that it consists of only nine feasible execution paths, despite of the fact that it contains three "for" loops and six "if" statements. Furthermore, it was found that all the path subprograms can be greatly simplified to explicate the function of the program.

The program in Example A.4 is a stack class. It is used to illustrate how the present method can be applied to an object-oriented program.

To make it easier to follow the steps taken in analysis, a pair of program texts listed side by side is used to show what is done in each step. One or more rules could be applied to the statements on the left-hand side. Arrows on the left margin mark the statements directly involved. The resulting text is listed on the right-hand side, with all added or altered statements printed in boldface type, and deleted statements are stricken through. Each pair is followed by an explanation of the rules used and the rationale behind that step, if appropriate. The text on the right-hand side is then copied to the left-hand side of the next pair to become the source of the next step.

Example A.1

Program A.1

```
include <iostream>
using namespace std;
int atoi(string& s)
{
  int i, n, sign;
  i = 0;
  while (isspace(s[i]))
    i = i + 1;
  if (s[i] == '-')
    sign = -1;
  else
    sign = 1;
  if (s[i] == '+' || s[i] == '-')
    i = i + 1;
  n = 0;
  while (isdigit(s[i])) {
    n = 10 * n + (s[i] - '0');
    i = i + 1;
  }
  return sign * n;
}
```

$\Rightarrow$

```
int atoi(string& s)
{
  int i, n, sign;
    i = 0;
  /\!(isspace(s[i]));
  while (isspace(s[i]))
    i = i + 1;
  /\!(s[i] == '-');
  if (s[i] == '-')
    sign = -1;
  else
    sign = 1;
  /\!(s[i] == '+' || s[i] == '-');
  if (s[i] == '+' || s[i] == '-')
    i = i + 1;
  n = 0;
  /\ (isdigit(s[i]));
  while (isdigit(s[i])) {
    n = 10 * n + (s[i] - '0');
    i = i + 1;
  }
  return sign * n;
}
```

Appendix A

Function atoi is a C++ version of the standard library routine that accepts a string of digits as input and returns the integer value in base 10 denoted by that input string. Thus, if the input is a single digit '7', atoi will assume the decimal integer value of seven, and if the input is a string of three digits, say, a '7' followed by a '6' and then a '5', atoi will assume the decimal integer value of 765 on completion of the execution.

In this example, constraints were inserted into the program to force the execution to proceed along a particular path that includes a loop at the end.

```
⇔
int atoi(string& s)
{
 int i, n, sign;
 i = 0;
 /\!(isspace(s[i]));
 while (isspace(s[i]))
   i = i + 1;
 /\!(s[i] == '-');
 if (s[i] == '-')
   sign = -1;
 else
   sign = 1;
 /\!(s[i] == '+' || s[i] == '-');
 if (s[i] == '+' || s[i] == '-')
   i = i + 1;
 n = 0;
 /\ (isdigit(s[i]));
→while (isdigit(s[i])) {
→   n = 10 * n + (s[i] - '0');
→   i = i + 1;
→}
 return sign * n;
 }
```

```
⇔
int atoi(string& s)
{
 int i, n, sign;

 i = 0;
 /\!(isspace(s[i]));
 while (isspace(s[i]))
   i = i + 1;
 /\!(s[i] == '-');
 if (s[i] == '-')
   sign = -1;
 else
   sign = 1;
 /\!(s[i] == '+' || s[i] == '-');
 if (s[i] == '+' || s[i] == '-')
   i = i + 1;
 n = 0;
 /\ (isdigit(s[i]));
   n = 10 * n + (s[i] - '0');
   i = i + 1;
 while (isdigit(s[i])) {
   n = 10 * n + (s[i] - '0');
   i = i + 1;
 }
 return sign * n;
 }
```

Corollaries 3.5 and 3.2 are applied to the relevant statements.

```
⇔                                        ⇒
int atoi(string& s)                      int atoi(string& s)
 {                                        {
   int i, n, sign;                          int i, n, sign;
   i = 0;
   /\!(isspace(s[i]));                      i = 0;
   /\!(s[i] == '-');                        /\!(isspace(s[i]));
   sign = 1;                                /\!(s[i] == '-');
   /\!(s[i] == '+' || s[i] == '-');         sign = 1;
   n = 0;                                   /\!(s[i] == '+' || s[i] == '-');
   /\ (isdigit(s[i]));                      n = 0;
   n = 10 * n + (s[i] - '0');               /\ (isdigit(s[i]));
   i = i + 1;                               n = 10 * n + (s[i] - '0');
→ while (isdigit(s[i])) {                   i = i + 1;
→   n = 10 * n + (s[i] - '0');             /\!(isdigit(s[i]));
→   i = i + 1;                             while (isdigit(s[i])) {
→ }                                            n = 10 * n + (s[i] - '0');
   return sign * n;                            i = i + 1;
 }                                         }
                                           return sign * n;
                                         }
```

Now suppose we wish to have the while loop iterated only once. The constraint is inserted to produce this effect.

```
⇔                                        ⇒
int atoi(string& s)                      int atoi(string& s)
 {                                        {
   int i, n, sign;                          int i, n, sign;
   i = 0;                                   i = 0;
   /\!(isspace(s[i]));                      /\!(isspace(s[i]));
   /\!(s[i] == '-');                        /\!(s[i] == '-');
   sign = 1;                                sign = 1;
   /\!(s[i] == '+' || s[i] == '-');         /\!(s[i] == '+' || s[i] == '-');
   n = 0;                                   n = 0;
   /\ (isdigit(s[i]));                      /\ (isdigit(s[i]));
   n = 10 * n + (s[i] - '0');               n = 10 * n + (s[i] - '0');
   i = i + 1;                               i = i + 1;
→ /\!(isdigit(s[i]));                       /\!(isdigit(s[i]));
→ while (isdigit(s[i])) {                   while (isdigit(s[i])) {
→ n = 10 * n + (s[i] - '0');                   n = 10 * n + (s[i] - '0');
→ i = i + 1;                                   i = i + 1;
→ }                                        }
   return sign * n;                        return sign * n;
 }                                        }
```

The basis for this step: Corollary 3.5.

Appendix A

⇔
```
int atoi(string& s)
{
  int i, n, sign;
  i = 0;
→ /\!(isspace(s[i]));
→ /\!(s[i] == '-');
  sign = 1;
  /\!(s[i] == '+' || s[i] == '-');
  n = 0;
  /\ (isdigit(s[i]));
  n = 10 * n + (s[i] - '0');
  i = i + 1;
  /\!(isdigit(s[i]));
  return sign * n;
}
```

⇒
```
int atoi(string& s)
{
  int i, n, sign;
  i = 0;
  /\!(isspace(s[i]))&&!(s[i]=='-');
  sign = 1;
  /\!(s[i] == '+' || s[i] == '-');
  n = 0;
  /\ (isdigit(s[i]));
  n = 10 * n + (s[i] - '0');
  i = i + 1;
  /\!(isdigit(s[i]));
  return sign * n;
}
```

The basis for this step: Corollary 3.8.

⇔
```
int atoi(string& s)
{
  int i, n, sign;
→ i = 0;
→ /\!(isspace(s[i]))&&!(s[i]=='-');
  sign = 1;
  /\!(s[i] == '+' || s[i] == '-');
  n = 0;
  /\ (isdigit(s[i]));
  n = 10 * n + (s[i] - '0');
  i = i + 1;
  /\!(isdigit(s[i]));
  return sign * n;
}
```

⇔
```
int atoi(string& s)
{
  int i, n, sign;
  /\!(isspace(s[0]))&&!(s[0]=='-');
  i = 0;
  sign = 1;
  /\!(s[i] == '+' || s[i] == '-');
  n = 0;
  /\ (isdigit(s[i]));
  n = 10 * n + (s[i] - '0');
  i = i + 1;
  /\!(isdigit(s[i]));
  return sign * n;
}
```

The basis for this step: Theorem 3.7.

```
⇔                                        ⇔
int atoi(string& s)                      int atoi(string& s)
{                                        {
  int i, n, sign;                          int i, n, sign;
  /\!(isspace(s[0]))&&!(s[0]=='-');        /\!(isspace(s[0]))&&!(s[0]=='-');
→ i = 0;                                   /\!(s[0] == '+' || s[0] == '-');
→ sign = 1;                                i = 0;
→ /\!(s[i] == '+' || s[i] == '-');        sign = 1;
  n = 0;                                   n = 0;
  /\ (isdigit(s[i]));                      /\ (isdigit(s[i]));
  n = 10 * n + (s[i] - '0');              n = 10 * n + (s[i] - '0');
  i = i + 1;                               i = i + 1;
  /\!(isdigit(s[i]));                      /\!(isdigit(s[i]));
  return sign * n;                         return sign * n;
}                                        }
```

The basis for this step: Theorem 3.7.

```
⇔                                        ⇔
int atoi(string& s)                      int atoi(string& s)
{                                        {
  int i, n, sign;                          int i, n, sign;
  /\!(isspace(s[0]))&&!(s[0]=='-');        /\!(isspace(s[0]))&&!(s[0]=='-');
  /\!(s[0] == '+' || s[0] == '-');        /\!(s[0] == '+' || s[0] == '-');
→ i = 0;                                   /\ (isdigit(s[0]));
→ sign = 1;                                i = 0;
→ n = 0;                                   sign = 1;
→ /\ (isdigit(s[i]));                      n = 0;
  n = 10 * n + (s[i] - '0');              n = 10 * n + (s[i] - '0');
  i = i + 1;                               i = i + 1;
  /\!(isdigit(s[i]));                      /\!(isdigit(s[i]));
  return sign * n;                         return sign * n;
}                                        }
```

The rule used in this step: Theorem 3.7.

Appendix A

```
⇔
int atoi(string& s)
 {
  int i, n, sign;
  /\!(isspace(s[0]))&&!(s[0]=='-');
  /\!(s[0] == '+' || s[0] == '-');
  /\ (isdigit(s[0]));
→i = 0;
→sign = 1;
→n = 0;
→n = 10 * n + (s[i] - '0');
→i = i + 1;
→/\!(isdigit(s[i]));
  return sign * n;
 }
```

```
⇔
int atoi(string& s)
 {
  int i, n, sign;
  /\!(isspace(s[0]))&&!(s[0]=='-');
  /\!(s[0] == '+' || s[0] == '-');
  /\ (isdigit(s[0]));
  /\!(isdigit(s[1]));
  i = 0;
  sign = 1;
  n = 0;
  n = 10 * n + (s[i] - '0');
  i = i + 1;
  return sign * n;
 }
```

The rule used in this step: Theorem 3.7.

```
⇔
int atoi(string& s)
 {
  int i, n, sign;
→/\!(isspace(s[0]))&&!(s[0]=='-');
→/\!(s[0] == '+' || s[0] == '-');
→/\ (isdigit(s[0]));
→/\!(isdigit(s[1]));
  i = 0;
  sign = 1;
  n = 0;
  n = 10 * n + (s[i] - '0');
  i = i + 1;
  return sign * n;
 }
```

```
⇔
int atoi(string& s)
 {
  int i, n, sign;
  /\(isdigit(s[0]))&&!(isdigit(s[1]));
  i = 0;
  sign = 1;
  n = 0;
  n = 10 * n + (s[i] - '0');
  i = i + 1;
  return sign * n;
 }
```

Logical simplification is performed.

```
⇔                                          ⇔
int atoi(string& s)                        int atoi(string& s)
 {                                          {
  int i, n, sign;                            int i, n, sign;
  /\(isdigit(s[0]))&&!(isdigit(s[1]));       /\(isdigit(s[0]))&&!(isdigit(s[1]));
  i = 0;                                     i = 0;
  sign = 1;                                  sign = 1;
→ n = 0;                                     n = 10 * 0 + (s[i] - '0');
→ n = 10 * n + (s[i] - '0');                 i = i + 1;
  i = i + 1;                                 return sign * n;
  return sign * n;                          }
 }
```

Corollary 3.10 is used to eliminate the assignment statement n = 0.

```
⇔                                          ⇔
int atoi(string& s)                        int atoi(string& s)
 {                                          {
  int i, n, sign;                            int i, n, sign;
  /\(isdigit(s[0]))&&!(isdigit(s[1]));       /\(isdigit(s[0]))&&!(isdigit(s[1]));
  i = 0;                                     i = 0;
  n = (s[i] - '0');                          n = (s[i] - '0');
→ sign = 1;                                  i = i + 1;
→ i = i + 1;                                 sign = 1;
  return sign * n;                           return sign * n;
 }                                          }
```

Corollary 3.11 is applied to interchange the two statements.

Appendix A

```
⇔
int atoi(string& s)
{
  int i, n, sign;
  /\(isdigit(s[0]))&&!(isdigit(s[1]));
  i = 0;
  n = (s[i] - '0');
  i = i + 1;
→ sign = 1;
→ return sign * n;
}
```
```
⇔
int atoi(string& s)
{
  int i, n, sign;
  /\(isdigit(s[0]))&&!(isdigit(s[1]));
  i = 0;
  n = (s[i] - '0');
  i = i + 1;
  return 1 * n;
}
```

Corollary 3.13 is used in this step.

```
⇔
int atoi(string& s)
{
  int i, n, sign;
  /\(isdigit(s[0]))&&!(isdigit(s[1]));
→ i = 0;
→ n = (s[i] - '0');
  i = i + 1;
  return n;
}
```
```
⇔
int atoi(string& s)
{
  int i, n, sign;
  /\(isdigit(s[0]))&&!(isdigit(s[1]));
  n = (s[0] - '0');
  i = 0;
  i = i + 1;
  return n;
}
```

Corollary 3.11 is applied here.

```
⇔                                          ⇔
int atoi(string& s)                        int atoi(string& s)
 {                                          {
   int i, n, sign;                            int i, n, sign;
   /\(isdigit(s[0]))&&!(isdigit(s[1]));       /\(isdigit(s[0]))&&!(isdigit(s[1]));
   n = (s[0] - '0');                          n = (s[0] - '0');
→ i = 0;                                      i = 1;
→ i = i + 1;                                   return n;
   return n;                                 }
 }
```

Corollary 3.10 is used to obtain this result.

```
⇔                                          ⇔
int atoi(string& s)                        int atoi(string& s)
 {                                          {
   int i, n, sign;                            int i, n, sign;
   /\(isdigit(s[0]))&&!(isdigit(s[1]));       /\(isdigit(s[0]))&&!(isdigit(s[1]));
   n = (s[0] - '0');                          n = (s[0] - '0');
→ i = 1;                                       return n;
→ return n;                                    i = 1;
 }                                          }
```

Corollary 3.13 is the basis for this transformation.

```
⇔                                          ⇔
int atoi(string& s)                        int atoi(string& s)
 {                                          {
   int i, n, sign;                            int i, n, sign;
   /\(isdigit(s[0]))&&!(isdigit(s[1]));       /\(isdigit(s[0]))&&!(isdigit(s[1]));
→ n = (s[0] - '0');                            return (s[0] - '0');
→ return n;                                    n = (s[0] - '0');
 }                                          }
```

Corollary 3.13 is applied in this step.

Appendix A

Thus we have shown that

```
int atoi(string& s)
{
  int i, n, sign;
  i = 0;
  /\!(isspace(s[i]));
  /\!(s[i] == '-');
  sign = 1;
  /\!(s[i] == '+' || s[i] == '-');
  n = 0;
  /\ (isdigit(s[i]));
  n = 10 * n + (s[i] - '0');
  i = i + 1;
  /\!(isdigit(s[i]));
  while (isdigit(s[i])) {
    n = 10 * n + (s[i] - '0');
    i = i + 1;
  }
  return sign * n;
}
```

⇔

```
int atoi(string& s)
{
  int i, n, sign;
  /\(isdigit(s[0]))&&!(isdigit(s[1]));
  return (s[0] - '0');
}
```

Example A.2

To be analyzed is a C++ program that computes the so–called 91–function (Manna, 1974), which can be defined as **if** $x \leq 100$ **then** $z := 91$ **else** $z := x - 10$.

Program A.2

```
#include <iostream>
using namespace std;
int main()
  {
   int x, y, z;
   cin >> x;
   y = 1;
   while (x <= 100) {
     x = x + 11;
     y = y + 1;
   }
   while (y!= 1) {
     x = x - 10;
     y = y - 1;
   while (x <= 100) {
     x = x + 11;
     y = y + 1;
     }
   }
   z = x - 10;
   cout << "z = " << z << endl;
  }
```

```
⇔ int main()
  {
   int x, y, z;
   cin >> x;
   y = 1;
   /\ x <= 100 || x > 100;
   while (x <= 100) {
     x = x + 11;
     y = y + 1;
   }
   while (y!= 1) {
     x = x - 10;
     y = y - 1;
     while (x <= 100) {
       x = x + 11;
       y = y + 1;
     }
   }
   z = x - 10;
   cout << "z = " << z << endl;
  }
```

By virtue of Corollary 4.8 we may insert a tautological constraint as shown on the right-hand side.

Tautological constraints in a program allow us to simplify or to transform the program. Therefore, as a general rule, we start by inserting as many tautological constraints as possible into part of the source code being examined. We then apply appropriate rules to rewrite the program. Once the rules have been applied, the tautological constraints will no longer be needed, and thus can be discarded. For this reason, it is useful to mark a tautological constraint in some way (e.g., underline it in handwriting). Henceforth a tautological constraint is given in italics.

Appendix A

```
⇔ int main()                            ⇔ int main()
 {                                       {
  int x, y, z;                            int x, y, z;

  cin >> x;                               cin >> x;
  y = 1;                                  y = 1;
→ /\ x <= 100 || x > 100;                 {{{
→ while (x <= 100) {                        /\ x <= 100;
→    x = x + 11;                            while (x <= 100) {
→    y = y + 1;                               x = x + 11;
  }                                           y = y + 1;
  while (y!= 1) {                           }
    x = x - 10;                             ...
    y = y - 1;                             /\ x > 100;
    while (x <= 100) {                      while (x <= 100) {
      x = x + 11;                             x = x + 11;
      y = y + 1;                              y = y + 1;
    }                                       }}}
  }                                       while (y!= 1) {
  z = x - 10;                               x = x - 10;
  cout << "z = " << z << endl;              y = y - 1;
 }                                          while (x <= 100) {
                                              x = x + 11;
                                              y = y + 1;
                                            }
                                          }
                                          z = x - 10;
                                          cout << "z = " << z << endl;
                                         }
```

Again, by virtue of Corollaries 4.8 and 3.5, we can rewrite the program as just shown.

```
⇔ int main()
{
  int x, y, z;
  cin >> x;
  y = 1;
  {{{
    /\ x <= 100;
    while (x <= 100) {
      x = x + 11;
      y = y + 1;
    }
    ...
    /\ x > 100;
  }}}
  while (y!= 1) {
    x = x - 10;
    y = y - 1;
    while (x <= 100) {
      x = x + 11;
      y = y + 1;
    }
  }
  z = x - 10;
  cout << "z = " << z << endl;
}
```

```
⇔
{{{
  int main()
  {
    int x, y, z;
    cin >> x;
    y = 1;
    /\ x <= 100;
    while (x <= 100) {
      x = x + 11;
      y = y + 1;
    }
    while (y!= 1) {
      x = x - 10;
      y = y - 1;
      while (x <= 100) {
        x = x + 11;
        y = y + 1;
      }
    }
    z = x - 10;
    cout << "z = " << z << endl;
  }
  ...
  int main()
  {
    int x, y, z;
    cin >> x;
    y = 1;
    /\ x > 100;
    while (y!= 1) {
      x = x - 10;
      y = y - 1;
      while (x <= 100) {
        x = x + 11;
        y = y + 1;
      }
    }
    z = x - 10;
    cout << "z = " << z << endl;
  }
}}}
```

Corollary 4.4, Part a, and Corollary 4.4, Part b are the basis for this step.

In the preceding we decomposed Program A.2 into a set of two subprograms, viz., Program A.2 = {Program A.2.1, Program A.2.2}. We simplify these two subprograms separately in the following program.

Appendix A

Program A.2.1

```
  cin >> x;
→ y = 1;
  /\ x <= 100;
  while (x <= 100) {
    x = x + 11;
    y = y + 1;
  }
  while (y!= 1) {
    x = x - 10;
    y = y - 1;
    while (x <= 100) {
      x = x + 11;
      y = y + 1;
    }
  }
  z = x - 10;
  cout << "z = " << z << endl;
```

```
  ⇔ cin >> x;
    y = 1;
    /\ y == 1;
    /\ x <= 100;
    while (x <= 100) {
      x = x + 11;
      y = y + 1;
    }
    while (y!= 1) {
      x = x - 10;
      y = y - 1;
      while (x <= 100) {
        x = x + 11;
        y = y + 1;
      }
    }
    z = x - 10;
    cout << "z = " << z << endl;
```

First, Corollary 6.1 is used to find a tautological constraint for the first loop, as just indicated.

```
  ⇔ cin >> x;
    y = 1;
→ /\ y == 1;
→ /\ x <= 100;
→ while (x <= 100) {
→   x = x + 11;
→   y = y + 1;
→ }
    while (y!= 1) {
      x = x - 10;
      y = y - 1;
      while (x <= 100) {
        x = x + 11;
        y = y + 1;
      }
    }
    z = x - 10;
    cout << "z = " << z << endl;
```

```
  ⇔ cin >> x;
    y = 1;
    /\ y == 1;
    /\ x <= 100;
    while (x <= 100) {
      x = x + 11;
      y = y + 1;
    }
    /\ x > 100;
    /\ x <= 111;
    /\ y!= 1;
    while (y!= 1) {
      x = x - 10;
      y = y - 1;
      while (x <= 100) {
        x = x + 11;
        y = y + 1;
      }
    }
    z = x - 10;
    cout << "z = " << z << endl;
```

Next, by virtue of Corollary 6.3 and Theorems 6.9 and 6.10, we insert the constraints $/\backslash$ x $>$ 100, $/\backslash$ x $<=$ 111, and $/\backslash$ y $!=$ 1. The constraint $/\backslash$ y $==$ 1 can now be discarded because it is no longer of any use.

```
⟺ cin >> x;                          ⟺ cin >> x;
  y = 1;                               y = 1;
  /\ x <= 100;                         /\ x <= 100;
  while (x <= 100) {                   while (x <= 100) {
    x = x + 11;                          x = x + 11;
    y = y + 1;                           y = y + 1;
  }                                    }
  /\ x > 100;                          /\ x > 100;
  /\ x <= 111;                         /\ x <= 111;
  /\ y!= 1;                            /\ y!= 1;
  while (y!= 1) {                      while (y!= 1) {
    x = x - 10;                          x = x - 10;
    y = y - 1;                           y = y - 1;
→   while (x <= 100) {                   while (x <= 100) {
→     x = x + 11;                          x = x + 11;
→     y = y + 1;                           y = y + 1;
→   }                                    }
  }                                    /\ x > 100;
  z = x - 10;                        }
  cout << "z = " << z << endl;       z = x - 10;
                                     cout << "z = " << z << endl;
```

By virtue of Corollary 6.3 we now insert $/\backslash$ x $>$ 100 at the end of the third loop.

```
⇔ cin >> x;                          ⇔ cin >> x;
  y = 1;                               y = 1;
  /\ x <= 100;                         /\ x <= 100;
  while (x <= 100) {                   while (x <= 100) {
    x = x + 11;                          x = x + 11;
    y = y + 1;                           y = y + 1;
  }                                    }
→ /\ x > 100;                          /\ x > 100;
→ /\ x <= 111;                         /\ x <= 111;
→ /\ y!= 1;                            /\ y!= 1;
→ while (y!= 1) {                      while (y!= 1) {
→   x = x - 10;                          /\ x > 100;
→   y = y - 1;                           x = x - 10;
→   while (x <= 100) {                   y = y - 1;
→     x = x + 11;                        while (x <= 100) {
→     y = y + 1;                           x = x + 11;
→   }                                      y = y + 1;
→   /\ x > 100;                          }
→ }                                      /\ x > 100;
  z = x - 10;                          }
  cout << "z = " << z << endl;         z = x - 10;
                                       cout << "z = " << z << endl;
```

Note that the condition $x > 100$ is true just before the second loop, and is also true at the end of its loop body, and therefore it is an invariant of this loop. Thus, by virtue of Theorem 6.7, it is a tautological constraint at the beginning of the loop body as well.

```
⇔ cin >> x;                                    ⇔ cin >> x;
  y = 1;                                         y = 1;
  /\ x <= 100;                                   /\ x <= 100;
  while (x <= 100) {                             while (x <= 100) {
    x = x + 11;                                    x = x + 11;
    y = y + 1;                                     y = y + 1;
  }                                              }
  /\ x > 100;                                    /\ x > 100;
  /\ x <= 111;                                   /\ x <= 111;
  /\ y!= 1;                                      /\ y!= 1;
  while (y!= 1) {                                while (y!= 1) {
    /\ x > 100;                                    /\ x > 100;
    x = x - 10;                                    x = x - 10;
    y = y - 1;                                     y = y - 1;
→   while (x <= 100) {                            /\ x <= 100 || x > 100;
→     x = x + 11;                                 while (x <= 100) {
→     y = y + 1;                                    x = x + 11;
→   }                                               y = y + 1;
→   /\ x > 100;                                   }
  }                                               /\ x > 100;
  z = x - 10;                                   }
  cout << "z = " << z << endl;                  z = x - 10;
                                                cout << "z = " << z << endl;
```

Observe that the third loop is identical to the first one. If we preconstrain it with $x <= 100$, it may help us find the loop invariant of the second loop, which may in turn help us find a way to simplify it. To that end, we now insert a tautological constraint, as just shown, as allowed by Corollary 4.8.

Appendix A

```
⇔ cin >> x;                              ⇔    cin >> x;
    y = 1;                                    y = 1;
    /\ x <= 100;                              /\ x <= 100;
    while (x <= 100) {                        while (x <= 100) {
      x = x + 11;                               x = x + 11;
      y = y + 1;                                y = y + 1;
    }                                         }
    /\ x > 100;                               /\ x > 100;
    /\ x <= 111;                              /\ x <= 111;
    /\ y!= 1;                                 /\ y!= 1;
    while (y!= 1) {                           while (y!= 1) {
→     /\ x > 100;                               {{{
→     x = x - 10;                                 /\ x > 100;
→     y = y - 1;                                  x = x - 10;
→     /\ x <= 100 ‖ x > 100;                      y = y - 1;
→     while (x <= 100) {                          /\ x <= 100;
→       x = x + 11;                               while (x <= 100) {
→       y = y + 1;                                  x = x + 11;
→     }                                             y = y + 1;
→     /\ x > 100;                                 }
    }                                             /\ x > 100;
    z = x - 10;                                 }}}
    cout << "z = " << z << endl;             }
                                            z = x - 10;
                                            cout << "z = " << z << endl;
```

The loop body of the second loop is decomposed into two subprograms.

Note that, if a constraint is tautological and is formed by use of disjunctive connectives, its components are not necessarily tautological. That is the reason why the constraints /\x <= 100 and /\x > 100 on the right-hand side are not expressed in italics.

```
⇔   cin >> x;                      ⇔   cin >> x;
    y = 1;                             y = 1;
    /\ x <= 100;                       /\ x <= 100;
    while (x <= 100) {                 while (x <= 100) {
        x = x + 11;                        x = x + 11;
        y = y + 1;                         y = y + 1;
    }                                  }
    /\ x > 100;                        /\ x > 100;
    /\ x <= 111;                       /\ x <= 111;
    /\ y!= 1;                          /\ y!= 1;
    while (y!= 1) {                    while (y!= 1) {
        {{{                                {{{
            /\ x > 100;                        /\ x > 100;
            x = x - 10;                        x = x - 10;
            y = y - 1;                         y = y - 1;
            /\ x <= 100;                       /\ x <= 100;
            while (x <= 100) {                 while (x <= 100) {
                x = x + 11;                        x = x + 11;
                y = y + 1;                         y = y + 1;
            }                                  }
            /\ x > 100;                        /\ x > 100;
        ...                                ...
            /\ x > 100;                        /\ x > 100;
            x = x - 10;                        x = x - 10;
            y = y - 1;                         y = y - 1;
→           /\ x > 100;                        /\ x > 100;
→           while (x <= 100) {                 while (x <= 100) {
→               x = x + 11;                        x = x + 11;
→               y = y + 1;                         y = y + 1;
→           }                                  }
            /\ x > 100;                        /\ x > 100;
        }}}                                }}}
    }                                  }
    z = x - 10;                        z = x - 10;
    cout << "z = " << z << endl;       cout << "z = " << z << endl;
```

The inner loop in the second subprogram can be dropped because it will
never be executed (Corollary 3.5).

```
⇔   cin >> x;
    y = 1;
    /\ x <= 100;
    while (x <= 100) {
        x = x + 11;
        y = y + 1;
    }
    /\ x > 100;
    /\ x <= 111;
    /\ y! = 1;
    while (y! = 1) {
        {{{
            /\ x > 100;
            x = x - 10;
            y = y - 1;
→           /\ x <= 100;
→           while (x <= 100) {
→               x = x + 11;
→               y = y + 1;
→           }
→           /\ x > 100;
        ...
            /\ x > 100;
            x = x - 10;
            y = y - 1;
            /\ x > 100;
        }}}
    }
    z = x - 10;
    cout << "z = " << z << endl;
```

```
⇔   cin >> x;
    y = 1;
    /\ x <= 100;
    while (x <= 100) {
        x = x + 11;
        y = y + 1;
    }
    /\ x > 100;
    /\ x <= 111;
    /\ y! = 1;
    while (y! = 1) {
        {{{
            /\ x > 100;
            x = x - 10;
            y = y - 1;
            /\ x <= 100;
            x = x + 11;
            y = y + 1;
            while (x <= 100) {
                x = x + 11;
                y = y + 1;
            }
            /\ x > 100;
        ...
            /\ x > 100;
            x = x - 10;
            y = y - 1;
            /\ x > 100;
        }}}
    }
    z = x - 10;
    cout << "z = " << z << endl;
```

Corollary 3.4 is applied to the first subprogram to see if we can find additional information about the inner loop therein.

```
⇔ cin >> x;                              ⇔ cin >> x;
    y = 1;                                    y = 1;
    /\ x <= 100;                             /\ x <= 100;
    while (x <= 100) {                        while (x <= 100) {
        x = x + 11;                              x = x + 11;
        y = y + 1;                               y = y + 1;
    }                                         }
    /\ x > 100;                              /\ x > 100;
    /\ x <= 111;                             /\ x <= 111;
    /\ y! = 1;                               /\ y! = 1;
    while (y! = 1) {                          while (y! = 1) {
        {{{                                       {{{
            /\ x > 100;                               /\ x > 100;
→           x = x - 10;                               /\ x <= 110;
→           y = y - 1;                                x = x + 1;
→           /\ x <= 100;                              while (x <= 100) {
→           x = x + 11;                                   x = x + 11;
→           y = y + 1;                                    y = y + 1;
            while (x <= 100) {                        }
                x = x + 11;                           /\ x > 100;
                y = y + 1;                        ...
            }                                         /\ x > 100;
            /\ x > 100;                               x = x - 10;
        ...                                           y = y - 1;
            /\ x > 100;                               /\ x > 100;
            x = x - 10;                       }}}
            y = y - 1;                        }
            /\ x > 100;                       z = x - 10;
        }}}                                   cout << "z = " << z << endl;
    }
    z = x - 10;
    cout << "z = " << z << endl;
```

The code segment above the third loop is simplified.

Appendix A

```
⇔ cin >> x;                          ⇔ cin >> x;
    y = 1;                               y = 1;
    /\ x <= 100;                         /\ x <= 100;
    while (x <= 100) {                   while (x <= 100) {
      x = x + 11;                          x = x + 11;
      y = y + 1;                           y = y + 1;
    }                                    }
    /\ x > 100;                          /\ x > 100;
    /\ x <= 111;                         /\ x <= 111;
    /\ y!= 1;                            /\ y!= 1;
    while (y!= 1) {                      while (y!= 1) {
      {{{                                  {{{
→       /\ x > 100;                          /\ x > 100;
        /\ x <= 110;                         /\ x <= 110;
→       x = x + 1;                           x = x + 1;
        while (x <= 100) {                   /\ x > 101;
          x = x + 11;                        while (x <= 100) {
          y = y + 1;                           x = x + 11;
        }                                      y = y + 1;
        /\ x > 100;                          }
        ...                                  /\ x > 100;
        /\ x > 100;                          ...
        x = x - 10;                          /\ x > 100;
        y = y - 1;                           x = x - 10;
        /\ x > 100;                          y = y - 1;
      }}}                                    /\ x > 100;
    }                                      }}}
    z = x - 10;                          }
    cout << "z = " << z << endl;         z = x - 10;
                                         cout << "z = " << z << endl;
```

Move the constraint $/\ x > 100$ downstream to see what has to be true just before the loop is entered.

```
⇔ cin >> x;                                    ⇔ cin >> x;
    y = 1;                                         y = 1;
    /\ x <= 100;                                   /\ x <= 100;
    while (x <= 100) {                             while (x <= 100) {
        x = x + 11;                                    x = x + 11;
        y = y + 1;                                     y = y + 1;
    }                                              }
    /\ x > 100;                                    /\ x > 100;
    /\ x <= 111;                                   /\ x <= 111;
    /\ y!= 1;                                      /\ y!= 1;
    while (y!= 1) {                                while (y!= 1) {
        {{{                                            {{{
            /\ x > 100;                                    /\ x > 100;
            /\ x <= 110;                                   /\ x <= 110;
            x = x + 1;                                     x = x + 1;
→           /\ x > 101;                                    /\ x > 101;
→           while (x <= 100) {                             while (x <= 100) {
→               x = x + 11;                                    x = x + 11;
→               y = y + 1;                                     y = y + 1;
→           }                                              }
            /\ x > 100;                                    /\ x > 100;
            ...                                            ...
            /\ x > 100;                                    /\ x > 100;
            x = x - 10;                                    x = x - 10;
            y = y - 1;                                     y = y - 1;
            /\ x > 100;                                    /\ x > 100;
        }}}                                            }}}
    }                                              }
    z = x - 10;                                    z = x - 10;
    cout << "z = " << z << endl;                   cout << "z = " << z << endl;
```

Obviously that loop will never be entered, and thus can be deleted.

Appendix A

```
⟺  cin >> x;
      y = 1;
      /\ x <= 100;
      while (x <= 100) {
         x = x + 11;
         y = y + 1;
      }
      /\ x > 100;
      /\ x <= 111;
      /\ y!= 1;
      while (y!= 1) {
         {{{
            /\ x > 100;
            /\ x <= 110;
            x = x + 1;
            /\ x > 100;

         . . .
            /\ x > 100;
→           x = x - 10;
→           y = y - 1;
→           /\ x > 100;
         }}}
      }
      z = x - 10;
      cout << "z = " << z << endl;
```

```
⟺  cin >> x;
      y = 1;
      /\ x <= 100;
      while (x <= 100) {
         x = x + 11;
         y = y + 1;
      }
      /\ x > 100;
      /\ x <= 111;
      /\ y!= 1;
      while (y!= 1) {
         {{{
            /\ x > 100;
            /\ x <= 110;
            x = x + 1;
            /\ x > 100;

         . . .
            /\ x > 100;
            /\ x > 110;
            x = x - 10;
            y = y - 1;
         }}}
      }
      z = x - 10;
      cout << "z = " << z << endl;
```

Move the constraint /\ x > 100 to the top.

```
⇔ cin >> x;                        ⇔ cin >> x;
    y = 1;                             y = 1;
    /\ x <= 100;                       /\ x <= 100;
    while (x <= 100) {                 while (x <= 100) {
        x = x + 11;                        x = x + 11;
        y = y + 1;                         y = y + 1;
    }                                  }
→   /\ x > 100;                        while (y!= 1) {
→   /\ x <= 111;                           {{{
→   /\ y!= 1;                                  /\ x <= 110;
    while (y!= 1) {                            x = x + 1;
        {{{                                    ...
→           /\ x > 100;                        /\ x > 110;
            /\ x <= 110;                        x = x - 10;
            x = x + 1;                          y = y - 1;
→           /\ x > 100;                    }}}
        ...                             }
→           /\ x > 100;                 z = x - 10;
            /\ x > 110;                 cout << "z = " << z << endl;
            x = x - 10;
            y = y - 1;
        }}}
    }
    z = x - 10;
    cout << "z = " << z << endl;
```

Note that we can also obtain this result by recomposing the loop construct from its symbolic trace, as shown in Chapter 7.

Appendix A

⟺ Program A.2.1.1

```
    cin >> x;
→   y = 1;
→   /\ x <= 100;
→   while (x <= 100) {
→      x = x + 11;
→      y = y + 1;
→   }
    while (y!= 1)
      {{{
         /\ x > 99
         /\ x <= 110;
         x = x + 1;
      ...
         /\ x > 110;
         x = x - 10;
         y = y - 1;
      }}}
    z = x - 10;
    cout << "z = " << z << endl;
```

⟺
```
    cin >> x;
    y = 1;
    /\ x <= 100;
    while (x <= 100) {
       x = x + 11;
       y = y + 1;
    }
    /\ x > 100;
    /\ x <= 111;
    /\ y!= 1;
    while (y!= 1)
      {{{
         /\ x > 99
         /\ x <= 110;
         x = x + 1;
      ...
         /\ x > 110;
         x = x - 10;
         y = y - 1;
      }}}
    z = x - 10;
    cout << "z = " << z << endl;
```

Three tautological constraints are inserted, as allowed by Corollary 6.3 and Theorems 6.9 and 6.10, respectively.

```
⇔  cin >> x;                          ⇔  cin >> x;
      y = 1;                                y = 1;
      /\ x <= 100;                          /\ x <= 100;
      while (x <= 100) {                    while (x <= 100) {
         x = x + 11;                            x = x + 11;
         y = y + 1;                             y = y + 1;
      }                                     }
→   /\ x > 100;                           /\ x > 100;
→   /\ x <= 111;                          /\ x <= 111;
→   /\ y!= 1;                             /\ y!= 1;
→   while (y!= 1)                         while (y!= 1)
→      {{{                                   /\ x > 100;
→         /\ x > 99                          /\ x <= 111;
→         /\ x <= 110;                       /\ y!= 1;
→         x = x + 1;                       {{{
→         ...                                 /\ x > 99
→         /\ x > 110;                         /\ x <= 110;
→         x = x - 10;                         x = x + 1;
→         y = y - 1;                       ...
→      }}}                                   /\ x > 110;
      z = x - 10;                            x = x - 10;
      cout << "z = " << z << endl;           y = y - 1;
                                          }}}
                                          z = x - 10;
                                          cout << "z = " << z << endl;
```

Three more tautological constraints are inserted. The first two are due to Theorem 6.7 and the last is due to Corollary 6.6.

```
⟺ cin >> x;                          ⟺ cin >> x;
    y = 1;                               y = 1;
    /\ x <= 100;                         /\ x <= 100;
    while (x <= 100) {                   while (x <= 100) {
      x = x + 11;                          x = x + 11;
      y = y + 1;                           y = y + 1;
    }                                    }
    /\ x > 100;                          /\ x > 100;
    /\ x <= 111;                         /\ x <= 111;
    /\ y != 1;                           /\ y != 1;
    while (y != 1)                       while (y != 1)
→     /\ x > 100;                          {{{
→     /\ x <= 111;                           /\ x > 100;
→     /\ y != 1;                             /\ x <= 111;
→     {{{                                    /\ y != 1;
→       /\ x > 99                            /\ x > 99
→       /\ x <= 110;                         /\ x <= 110;
→       x = x + 1;                           x = x + 1;
→     ...                                  ...
→       /\ x > 110;                          /\ x > 100;
→       x = x - 10;                          /\ x <= 111;
→       y = y - 1;                           /\ y != 1;
→     }}}                                    /\ x > 110;
    z = x - 10;                              x = x - 10;
    cout << "z = " << z << endl;            y = y - 1;
                                         }}}
                                         z = x - 10;
                                         cout << "z = " << z << endl;
```

This is done by virtue of Corollary 4.9.

```
⇔  cin >> x;                           ⇔  cin >> x;
     y = 1;                                 y = 1;
     /\ x <= 100;                           /\ x <= 100;
     while (x <= 100) {                     while (x <= 100) {
        x = x + 11;                            x = x + 11;
        y = y + 1;                             y = y + 1;
     }                                      }
     /\ x > 100;                            while (y != 1)
     /\ x <= 111;                              {{{
     /\ y != 1;                                   /\ x > 100;
     while (y != 1)                               /\ x <= 110;
        {{{                                       /\ y != 1;
→          /\ x > 100;                            x = x + 1;
→          /\ x <= 111;                        ...
→          /\ y != 1;                             /\ x == 111;
→          /\ x > 99                              /\ y != 1;
→          /\ x <= 110;                           x = x - 10;
→          x = x + 1;                             y = y - 1;
→          ...                                }}}
→          /\ x > 100;                      z = x - 10;
→          /\ x <= 111;                      cout << "z = " << z << endl;
→          /\ y != 1;
→          /\ x > 110;
→          x = x - 10;
→          y = y - 1;
        }}}
     z = x - 10;
     cout << "z = " << z << endl;
```

This is obtained through logical simplification of the loop body.

Appendix A

```
⇔ cin >> x;                          ⇔ cin >> x;
    y = 1;                               y = 1;
    /\ x <= 100;                         /\ x <= 100;
    while (x <= 100) {                   while (x <= 100) {
      x = x + 11;                          x = x + 11;
      y = y + 1;                           y = y + 1;
    }                                    }
    while (y != 1)                       while (y != 1)
        {{{                                  {{{
→         /\ x > 100;                        x = x + 1;
→         /\ x <= 110;                       /\ x > 101;
→         /\ y != 1;                         /\ x <= 111;
→         x = x + 1;                         /\ y != 1;
          ...                                ...
→         /\ x == 111;                       x = x - 10;
→         /\ y != 1;                         y = y - 1;
→         x = x - 10;                        /\ x == 101
→         y = y - 1;                         /\ y != 0;
        }}}                                }}}
    z = x - 10;                          z = x - 10;
    cout << "z = " << z << endl;         cout << "z = " << z << endl;
```

We obtain this by using Theorem 3.7 to move all constraints downstream.

```
⇔ cin >> x;                              ⇔ cin >> x;
   y = 1;                                   y = 1;
   /\ x <= 100;                             /\ x <= 100;
   while (x <= 100) {                       while (x <= 100) {
      x = x + 11;                              x = x + 11;
      y = y + 1;                               y = y + 1;
   }                                        }
   while (y != 1)                           while (y != 1) {
      {{{                                      {{{
         x = x + 1;                              x = x + 1;
→        /\ x > 101;                            /\ x > 101;
→        /\ x <= 111;                           /\ x <= 111;
→        /\ y != 1;                             /\ y != 1;
         ...                                     ...
         x = x - 10;                             x = x - 10;
         y = y - 1;                              y = y - 1;
→        /\ x == 101                             /\ x == 101
→        /\ y != 0;                              /\ y != 0;
      }}}                                      }}};
   z = x - 10;                               /\ (x > 101 && x <= 111
   cout << "z = " << z << endl;        && y != 1) || (x == 101
                                       && y != 0);
                                          }
                                          z = x - 10;
                                          cout << "z = " << z << endl;
```

By virtue of Corollary 4.10, we can move the constraints immediately outside of the loop body, as just shown.

Appendix A

```
⟺ cin >> x;                           ⟺ cin >> x;
    y = 1;                                y = 1;
    /\ x <= 100;                          /\ x <= 100;
    while (x <= 100) {                    while (x <= 100) {
       x = x + 11;                           x = x + 11;
       y = y + 1;                            y = y + 1;
    }                                     }
→ while (y != 1) {                       while (y != 1) {
→    {{{                                    {{{
→       x = x + 1;                             x = x + 1;
→       /\ x > 101;                            /\ x > 101;
→       /\ x <= 111;                           /\ x <= 111;
→       /\ y != 1;
→       ...                                    ...
→       x = x - 10;                            x = x - 10;
→       y = y - 1;                             y = y - 1;
→       /\ x == 101                            /\ x == 101
→       /\ y != 0;                          }}};
→    }}};                                   /\ (x > 101 && x <= 111 &&
→    /\ (x > 101 && x <= 111           y != 1) || (x == 101 && y != 0);
&& y != 1) || (x == 101                  }
&& y != 0);                               /\ (x > 101 && x <= 111
    }                                 && y != 1) || (x == 101 && y != 0);
    z = x - 10;                           /\ y == 1;
    cout << "z = " << z << endl;          z = x - 10;
                                          cout << "z = " << z << endl;
```

This is obtained by virtue of Corollaries 6.11 and 6.3.

```
⇔ cin >> x;                          ⇔ cin >> x;
    y = 1;                               y = 1;
    /\ x <= 100;                         /\ x <= 100;
    while (x <= 100) {                   while (x <= 100) {
        x = x + 11;                          x = x + 11;
        y = y + 1;                           y = y + 1;
    }                                    }
    while (y != 1) {                     while (y != 1) {
        {{{                                  {{{
            x = x + 1;                           x = x + 1;
            /\ x > 101;                          /\ x > 101;
            /\ x <= 111;                         /\ x <= 111;
            ...                                  ...
            x = x - 10;                          x = x - 10;
            y = y - 1;                           y = y - 1;
            /\ x == 101                          /\ x == 101
        }}};                                 }}};
    }                                    }
→   /\ (x > 101 && x <= 111           /\ ((x > 101 && x <= 111
&& y != 1) || (x == 101            && y != 1) || (x == 101
&& y != 0);                        && y != 0)) && y == 1;
    /\ y == 1;                           z = x - 10;
    z = x - 10;                          cout << "z = " << z << endl;
    cout << "z = " << z << endl;
```

The tautological constraint at the bottom of the loop body is dropped.

Appendix A

```
⇔ cin >> x;                          ⇔ cin >> x;
    y = 1;                               y = 1;
    /\ x <= 100;                         /\ x <= 100;
    while (x <= 100) {                   while (x <= 100) {
        x = x + 11;                          x = x + 11;
        y = y + 1;                           y = y + 1;
    }                                    }
    while (y != 1) {                     while (y != 1) {
        {{{                                  {{{
            x = x + 1;                           x = x + 1;
            /\ x > 101;                          /\ x > 101;
            /\ x <= 111;                         /\ x <= 111;
            ...                                  ...
            x = x - 10;                          x = x - 10;
            y = y - 1;                           y = y - 1;
            /\ x == 101                          /\ x == 101
        }}};                                 }}};
    }                                    }
→     /\ ((x > 101 && x <= 111         /\ x == 101 && y == 1;
&& y != 1) || (x == 101                z = x - 10;
&& y != 0)) && y == 1;                 cout << "z = " << z << endl;
    z = x - 10;
    cout << "z = " << z << endl;
```

The tautological constraint at the bottom of the loop is logically simplified.

```
⟺ cin >> x;                              ⟺ cin >> x;
    y = 1;                                   y = 1;
    /\ x <= 100;                             /\ x <= 100;
    while (x <= 100) {                       while (x <= 100) {
        x = x + 11;                              x = x + 11;
        y = y + 1;                               y = y + 1;
    }                                        }
    while (y != 1) {                         while (y != 1) {
        {{{                                      {{{
            x = x + 1;                               x = x + 1;
            /\ x > 101;                              /\ x > 101;
            /\ x <= 111;                             /\ x <= 111;
        ...                                      ...
            x = x - 10;                              x = x - 10;
            y = y - 1;                               y = y - 1;
            /\ x == 101                              /\ x == 101
        }}};                                     }}};
    }                                        }
→   /\ x == 101 && y == 1;                   /\ y == 1;
    z = x - 10;                              /\ x == 101;
    cout << "z = " << z << endl;             z = x - 10;
                                            cout << "z = " << z << endl;
```

The constraint is split in two by virtue of Corollary 3.8.

Appendix A

```
⇔ cin >> x;                              ⇔ cin >> x;
  y = 1;                                   y = 1;
  /\ x <= 100;                             /\ x <= 100;
  while (x <= 100) {                       while (x <= 100) {
    x = x + 11;                              x = x + 11;
    y = y + 1;                               y = y + 1;
  }                                        }
  while (y != 1) {                         while (y != 1) {
    {{{                                      {{{
      x = x + 1;                               x = x + 1;
      /\ x > 101;                              /\ x > 101;
      /\ x <= 111;                             /\ x <= 111;

      ...                                      ...
      x = x - 10;                              x = x - 10;
      y = y - 1;                               y = y - 1;
      /\ x == 101                              /\ x == 101
    }}};                                     }}};
  }                                        }
→ /\ y == 1;                             /\ y == 1;
→ /\ x == 101;                             /\ x == 101;
  z = x - 10;                              x = 101;
  cout << "z = " << z << endl;             z = x - 10;
                                           cout << "z = " << z << endl;
```

We can now discard the tautological constraint $/\!\backslash\ y\ ==\ 1$ and insert the assignment statement $x\ =\ 101$ by virtue of Corollary 6.1.

```
⇔ cin >> x;                          ⇔ cin >> x;
    y = 1;                               y = 1;
    /\ x <= 100;                         /\ x <= 100;
    while (x <= 100) {                   while (x <= 100) {
        x = x + 11;                          x = x + 11;
        y = y + 1;                           y = y + 1;
    }                                    }
    while (y != 1) {                     while (y != 1) {
        {{{                                  {{{
            x = x + 1;                           x = x + 1;
            /\ x > 101;                          /\ x > 101;
            /\ x <= 111;                         /\ x <= 111;
            ...                                  ...
            x = x - 10;                          x = x - 10;
            y = y - 1;                           y = y - 1;
            /\ x == 101                          /\ x == 101
        }}};                                 }}};
    }                                    }
→   x = 101;                             x = 101;
→   z = x - 10;                          z = 91;
    cout << "z = " << z << endl;         cout << "z = " << z << endl;
```

We can now discard the tautological constraint and simplify the last assignment statement by virtue of Corollary 3.13.

Appendix A

```
⇔ cin >> x;               ⇔ cin >> x;
  y = 1;                    /\ x <= 100;
  /\ x <= 100;              z = 91;
  while (x <= 100) {        cout << "z = " << z << endl;
    x = x + 11;
    y = y + 1;
  }
  while (y != 1) {
    {{{
      x = x + 1;
      /\ x > 101;
      /\ x <= 111;
    . . .
      x = x - 10;
      y = y - 1;
      /\ x == 101
    }}};
  }
  x = 101;
  z = 91;
  cout << "z = " << z << endl;
```

At this juncture any expression that does not contribute to the definition of this subprogram or computation of the value of the only output variable, z, can be deleted.

Next, we simplify S$_2$, which can be done readily, as subsequently shown.

Program A.2.2

```
    cin >> x;
→   y = 1;
    /\ x > 100;
    while (y != 1) {
        x = x - 10;
        y = y - 1;
        while (x <= 100) {
            x = x + 11;
            y = y + 1;
        }
    }
    z = x - 10;
    cout << "z = " << z << endl;
```

⇔
```
    cin >> x;
    y = 1;
    /\ y == 1;
    /\ x > 100;
    while (y != 1) {
        x = x - 10;
        y = y - 1;
        while (x <= 100) {
            x = x + 11;
            y = y + 1;
        }
    }
    z = x - 10;
    cout << "z = " << z << endl;
```

⇔
```
    cin >> x;
→   y = 1;
    /\ y == 1;
    /\ x > 100;
→   while (y != 1) {
→       x = x - 10;
→       y = y - 1;
→       while (x <= 100) {
→           x = x + 11;
→           y = y + 1;
→       }
→   }
    z = x - 10;
    cout << "z = " << z << endl;
```

⇔
```
    cin >> x;
    y = 1;
    /\ y == 1;
    /\ x > 100;
    z = x - 10;
    cout << "z = " << z << endl;
```

⇔
```
    cin >> x;
    y = 1;
    /\ y == 1;
    /\ x > 100;
    z = x - 10;
    cout << "z = " << z << endl;
```

⇔
```
    cin >> x;
    /\ x > 100;
    z = x - 10;
    cout << "z = " << z << endl;
```

Thus we have shown that we obtain Program A.2.

Appendix A

Program A.2

```
⇔  {Program A.2.1, Program A.2.2}
⇔  {{{
       cin >> x;
       /\ x <= 100;
       z = 91;
       cout << "z = " << z << endl;
       ...
       cin >> x;
       /\ x > 100;
       z = x - 10;
       cout << "z = " << z << endl;
   }}}

⇔  cin >> x;
      {{{
         /\ x <= 100;
         z = 91;
      ...
         /\ x > 100;
         z = x - 10;
      }}}
         cout << "z = " << z << endl;

⇔  cin >> x;
      if x <= 100
         z = 91;
      else
         z = x - 10;
      cout << "z = " << z << endl;
```

and therefore

Program A.2

```
#include <iostream>
using namespace std;
int main()
  {
    int x, y, z;
    cin >> x;
    y = 1;
    while (x <= 100) {
      x = x + 11;
      y = y + 1;
    }
    while (y != 1) {
      x = x - 10;
      y = y - 1;
        while (x <= 100) {
          x = x + 11;
          y = y + 1;
        }
    }
  z = x - 10;
  cout << "z = " << z << endl;
  }
```

⇔

```
#include <iostream>
using namespace std;
int main()
  {
    int x, y, z;
    cin >> x;
    if x <= 100
      z = 91;
    else
      z = x - 10;
    cout << "z = " << z << endl;
  }
```

The correctness of this program now becomes evident.

Example A.3

Consider the following program in C++.

Program A.3

```
#include <iostream>
#include <string>
using namespace std;

string getstring();

int main()
{
  string rfilename;
  rfilename = getstring();
  cout << rfilename << endl;
```

```
}
string getstring()
{
 string buf, buf1;
 int c1, c2, c3, j, k, k1, k2, n1, n2, testflag;
 char ch;
 c << "Enter the file name to be recoded:" << endl
 cin >> buf;
 buf.replace(0, buf.find('')+1, buf);
 if (buf.find(']') == npos)
   buf1 = "";
 else
   buf1 = buf.substr(0, buf.find(']')+1);
   buf.erase(0, buf.find(']'));
 if (buf.find('.')!= npos)
   buf = buf.substr(0, buf.find('.'));
 c1 = buf.length();
 if (c1 < 9) {
   c2 = 9 - c1;
   n1 = 9;
   n2 = c1;
   if (c1 < c2)
     testflag = 1;
 else {
   j = c1;
   c1 = c2;
   c2 = j;
   testflag = 0;
 }
 if (c1 == 0) {
   k1 = c2;
   k2 = c2;
 }
 else {
   k1 = c2 / c1;
   k2 = c2% c1;
 }
 buf[n1] = '\0';
```

```
for (k = 0; k < c1; ++k) {
  if (k2 == 0)
    c2 = k1;
  else {
    c2 = k1 + 1;
    -k2;
  }
  if (testflag)
    c3 = 1;
  else {
    c3 = c2;
    c2 = 1;
  }
  for (j = 0; j < c2; ++j) {
   buf[n1-1] = '9';
    -n1;
  }
  if (n1!= n2)
  for (j = 0; j < c3; ++j) {
      buf[n1-1] = buf[n2-1];
      -n1;
      -n2;
  }
 }
}
buf.insert(9, ".ABC");
buf.insert(0, buf1);
return buf;
}
```

The reader may wish to determine what this program does without reading the helpful information given in the following discussion. Tests in the past indicated that very few people could answer this question completely and correctly in half an hour or less.

The first part of the program is relatively easy to understand. The second part (printed in boldface type) is not. To facilitate understanding of the

Appendix A

second part, we shall use the present method to decompose it into a set of trace subprograms. An example of trace subprograms follows.

```
/\ c1 < 9;
c2 = 9 - c1;
n1 = 9;
n2 = c1;
/\ c1 < c2;
testflag = 1;
/\!(c1 == 0);
k1 = c2 / c1;
k2 = c2% c1;
buf[n1] = '\0';
k = 0;
/\ k < c1;
/\ k2 == 0;
c2 = k1;
/\ testflag;
c3 = 1;
j = 0;
/\ j < c2;
buf[n1-1] = '9';
n1 = n1 - 1;
j = j + 1;
/\ j < c2;
buf[n1-1] = '9';
n1 = n1 - 1;
j = j + 1;
/\!(j < c2);
/\ n1!= n2;
j = 0;
/\j < c3
buf[n1-1] = buf[n2-1];
n1 = n1 - 1;
n2 = n2 - 1;
j = j + 1;
/\!(j < c3);
k = k + 1;
```

```
/\ k < c1;
/\ k2 == 0;
c2 = k1;
/\ testflag;
c3 = 1;
j = 0;
/\ j < c2;
buf[n1-1] = '9';
n1 = n1 - 1;
j = j + 1;
/\ j < c2;
buf[n1-1] = '9';
n1 = n1 - 1;
j = j + 1;
/\!(j < c2);
buf[n1 - 1] = '9'
/\ n1!= n2;
j = 0;
/\j < c3
buf[n1-1] = buf[n2-1];
n1 = n1 - 1;
n2 = n2 - 1;
j = j + 1;
/\!(j < c3);
k = k + 1;
/\ k < c1;
/\ k2 == 0;
c2 = k1;
/\ testflag;
c3 = 1;
j = 0;
/\ j < c2;
buf[n1-1] = '9';
n1 = n1 - 1;
j = j + 1;
/\ j < c2;
buf[n1-1] = '9';
n1 = n1 - 1;
```

Appendix A

```
j = j + 1;
/\!(j < c2);
/\!(n1!= n2);
```

This trace subprogram can be readily simplified to this one:

```
⇔ /\ c1 == 3;
   buf[9] = '\0';
   buf[8] = '9';
   buf[7] = '9';
   buf[6] = buf[2];
   buf[5] = '9';
   buf[4] = '9';
   buf[3] = buf[1];
   buf[2] = '9';
   buf[1] = '9';
```

It turns out that the second part of the program can be decomposed into a set of only 10 trace subprograms, in spite of the fact that it contains six "if" statements and three "for" loops! Furthermore, each trace subprogram can be greatly simplified, as just exemplified.

In short, by using the present method to do decomposition and simplification of the second part, we can rewrite Program A.3 as shown in Program A.3.1

Program A.3.1

```
#include <iostream>
using namespace std;
string getstring();
int main()
{
  string rfilename;
  rfilename = getstring();
  cout << rfilename << endl;
}
string getstring()
```

```
{
 string buf, buf1;
 int c1, c2, c3, j, k, k1, k2, n1, n2, testflag;
 char ch;
 c << "Enter the file name to be recoded:" << endl
cin >> buf;
buf.replace(0, buf.find(' ')+1, buf);
if (buf.find(']') == npos)
 buf1 = "";
else
 buf1 = buf.substr(0, buf.find(']')+1);
 buf.erase(0, buf.find(']'));
if (buf.find('.')!= npos)
 buf = buf.substr(0, buf.find('.'));
c1 = buf.length();
{{{
 /\ c1 >= 9;
...
 /\ c1 == 0;
 buf[9] = '\0';
...
 /\ c1 == 1;
 buf[9] = '\0';
 buf[8] = '9';
 buf[7] = '9';
 buf[6] = '9';
 buf[5] = '9';
 buf[4] = '9';
 buf[3] = '9';
 buf[2] = '9';
 buf[1] = '9';
...
 /\ c1 == 2;
 buf[9] = '\0';
 buf[8] = '9';
 buf[7] = '9';
 buf[6] = '9';
 buf[5] = '9';
```

Appendix A

```
      buf[4]  =  buf[1];
      buf[3]  =  '9';
      buf[2]  =  '9';
      buf[1]  =  '9';
   ...
   /\ c1  ==  3;
      buf[9]  =  '\0';
      buf[8]  =  '9';
      buf[7]  =  '9';
      buf[6]  =  buf[2];
      buf[5]  =  '9';
      buf[4]  =  '9';
      buf[3]  =  buf[1];
      buf[2]  =  '9';
      buf[1]  =  '9';
   ...
   /\ c1  ==  4;
      buf[9]  =  '\0';
      buf[8]  =  '9';
      buf[7]  =  '9';
      buf[6]  =  buf[3];
      buf[5]  =  '9';
      buf[4]  =  buf[2];
      buf[3]  =  '9';
      buf[2]  =  buf[1];
      buf[1]  =  '9';
   ...
   /\ c1  ==  5;
      buf[9]  =  '\0';
      buf[8]  =  '9';
      buf[7]  =  buf[4];
      buf[6]  =  buf[3];
      buf[5]  =  '9';
      buf[4]  =  buf[2];
      buf[3]  =  '9';
      buf[2]  =  buf[1];
      buf[1]  =  '9';
   ...
```

```
      /\ c1 == 6;
      buf[9] = '\0';
      buf[8] = '9';
      buf[7] = buf[5];
      buf[6] = buf[4];
      buf[5] = '9';
      buf[4] = buf[3];
      buf[3] = buf[2];
      buf[2] = '9';
   ,,,
      /\ c1 == 7;
      buf[9] = '\0';
      buf[8] = '9';
      buf[7] = buf[6];
      buf[6] = buf[5];
      buf[5] = buf[4];
      buf[4] = buf[3];
      buf[3] = '9';
   ,,,
      /\ c1 == 8;
      buf[9] = '\0';
      buf[8] = '9';
   }}}
   buf.insert(9, ".ABC");
   buf.insert(0, buf1);
   return buf;
   }
```

The portion of Program A.3.1 printed in bold-face expresses the function to be performed by that part of the program in the most direct and understandable way. This equivalence transformation should be of great help to those who need to understand the program or to verify its correctness.

The program was written to reformat file descriptors required by a legacy software tool. An input file descriptor may consist of four fields:

Appendix A

[<drive name>]<file name>.<file type>;<version number>.

All fields, except the file name, are optional. The program reads a file descriptor in this format, truncates the file name to the length of nine if it is longer, and pads it with 9's if it is shorter, so that the length of the resulting file name is exactly nine. The padding must be done in such a way that the 9's are distributed as evenly as possible. Furthermore, it changes the file type to "ABC" and discards the version number. The drive name, if any, remains intact.

It is easy to see from Program A.3.1 that Program A.3 reformats input file descriptors, as previously described.

The first part of the program reads the input descriptor, stores the file name in array `buf`, stores the drive name, if any, in array `buf1`, and then assigns the length of the file name to variable `c1`. The file name is truncated if its length is greater than 9.

The second (highlighted) portion of the program makes the length of file name exactly equal to nine. It pads the input file name with 9's if its length is less than 9.

The remaining statements complete the construction of the output file descriptor by postfixing the file name with string ".ABC" and prefixing it with the drive name.

The analysis result represented by Program A.3.1 clearly reveals a flaw in the program. When the input file name is an empty string, variable `c1` is set to 0, and the program will take the first 9 characters in array `buf`, whatever that may be, as the file name, and proceed to construct the output file descriptor just as it does for other values of `c1`. This program behavior is acceptable only if it is an acceptable assumption that an empty string will never occur as a file name of any input file descriptor.

Example A.4

Consider the stack class in C++ listed below, which is adopted from Prata (2005). This example program is used to show that an execution of an object–oriented program will proceed along an execution path just like a procedure–oriented program, and the present method can be used to analyze the associated trace subprogram in a similar manner.

Program A.4.1

```
// stack.h - class definition for the stack ADT
#ifndef STACK_H_
#define STACK_H_
typedef char Item;
class Stack
{
private:
  enum {MAX = 10};              // constant specific
                               // to class
  Item items[MAX];             // holds stack items
  int top;                     // index for top
                               // stack item
public:
  Stack();
  bool isempty() const;
  bool isfull() const;
  // push() returns false if stack is already full,
  // true otherwise
  bool push(const Item & item); // add item to stack
  // pop() returns false if stack is already empty,
  // true otherwise
  bool pop(Item & item);       // pop top into item
};
#endif
```

Suppose the methods (member functions) are implemented as follows:

```
// stack.cpp - stack member functions
#include "stack.h"
Stack::Stack()               // create an empty stack
```

Appendix A

```cpp
{
 top = 0;
}
bool Stack::isempty() const
{
 return top == 0;
}
bool Stack::isfull() const
{
 return top == MAX;
}
bool Stack::push(const item & item)
{
 if (top < MAX)
 {
   items[top++] = item;
   return true;
 }
 else
   return false;
}
bool Stack::pop(item & item)
{
 if (top > 0)
 {
   item = items[-top]
   return true;
 }
 else
   return false}
}
```

Now if we test-execute Program A.4.1 by using the following test driver:

Program A.4.2

```cpp
// #includes and Stack declarations
int main()
```

```
{
 using namespace std;
 Stack xStack; // create an empty stack
 char ch
 cout << "Start testing..." << endl
 xStack.push('d');
 xStack.push('o');
 xStack.push('p');
 xStack.pop(ch);
 xStack.push('P');
 xStack.push ('i');
 if (xStack.full())
    cout << "Incorrect response!" << endl;
 cout << "Done!" << endl;
 return 0;
}
```

The execution will proceed along the execution path described by the following symbolic trace (listed on the left-hand side).

Appendix A

```
Stack xStack;                        Stack xStack;
top = 0;                             top = 0;
cout << "Start testing" << endl;     cout << "Start testing" << endl;
xStack.push('d');                    xStack.push('d');
/\ top < MAX;                        /\ top < MAX;
items[top++] = item;                 items[top++] = item;
return true;                         return true;
xStack.push('o');                    xStack.push('o');
/\ top < MAX;                        /\ top < MAX;
items[top++] = item;                 items[top++] = item;
return true;                         return true;
xStack.push('p');                    xStack.push('p');
/\ top < MAX;                        /\ top < MAX;
items[top++] = item;                 items[top++] = item;
return true;                         return true;
xStack.pop(ch);                      xStack.pop(ch);
/\ top > 0;                          /\ top > 0;
ch = items[-top]                     ch = items[-top]
return true;                         return true;
xStack.push('P');                    xStack.push('P');
/\ top < MAX;                        /\ top < MAX;
items[top++] = item;                 items[top++] = item;
return true;                         return true;
xStack.push('i');                    xStack.push('i');
/\ top < MAX;                        /\ top < MAX;
items[top++] = item;                 items[top++] = item;
return true;                         return true;
/\!(top == MAX);                     /\!(top == MAX);
cout << "Done!" << endl;             cout << "Done!" << endl;
return 0;                            return 0;
```

We first cross out all statements that are nonessential in understanding
the computation performed.

```
top = 0;                        ⇔
xStack.push('d');                   top = 0;
/\ top < MAX;                       item = 'd';
items[top++] = item;                /\ top < MAX;
xStack.push('o');                   items[top++] = item;
/\ top < MAX;                       item = 'o';
items[top++] = item;                /\ top < MAX;
xStack.push('p');                   items[top++] = item;
/\ top < MAX;                       item = 'p';
items[top++] = item;                /\ top < MAX;
xStack.pop(ch);                     items[top++] = item;
/\ top > 0;                         /\ top > 0;
ch = items[-top]                    ch = items[-top]
xStack.push('P');                   item = 'P';
/\ top < MAX;                       /\ top < MAX;
items[top++] = item;                items[top++] = item;
xStack.push('i');                   item = 'i';
/\ top < MAX;                       /\ top < MAX;
items[top++] = item;                items[top++] = item;
/\!(top == MAX);                    /\!(top == MAX);
return 0;                           return 0;
```

Appendix A

```
⇔
top = 0;
item = 'd';
/\ top < MAX;
items[top++] = item;
item = 'o';
/\ top < MAX;
items[top++] = item;
item = 'p';
/\ top < MAX;
items[top++] = item;
/\ top > 0;
ch = items[-top]
item = 'P';
/\ top < MAX;
items[top++] = item;
item = 'i';
/\ top < MAX;
items[top++] = item;
/\!(top == MAX);
return 0;
```

```
⇔
top = 0;
item = 'd';
/\ top < MAX;
items[top] = item;
top = top + 1;
item = 'o';
/\ top < MAX;
items[top] = item;
top = top + 1;
item = 'p';
/\ top < MAX;
items[top] = item;
top = top + 1;
/\ top > 0;
top = top - 1;
ch = items[top]
item = 'P';
/\ top < MAX;
items[top] = item;
top = top + 1;
item = 'i';
/\ top < MAX;
items[top] = item;
top = top + 1;
/\!(top == MAX);
return 0;
```

```
⇔                               ⇔
top = 0;                        /\ 0 < MAX;
item = 'd';                     /\ 1 < MAX;
/\ top < MAX;                   /\ 2 < MAX;
items[top] = item;              /\ 3 > 0;
top = top + 1;                  /\ 2 < MAX;
item = 'o';                     /\ 3 < MAX;
/\ top < MAX;                   /\!(4 == MAX);
items[top] = item;              top = 0;
top = top + 1;                  item = 'd';
item = 'p';                     items[top] = item;
/\ top < MAX;                   top = top + 1;
items[top] = item;              item = 'o';
top = top + 1;                  items[top] = item;
/\ top > 0;                     top = top + 1;
top = top - 1;                  item = 'p';
ch = items[top]                 items[top] = item;
item = 'P';                     top = top + 1;
/\ top < MAX;                   top = top - 1;
items[top] = item;              ch = items[top]
top = top + 1;                  item = 'P';
item = 'i';                     items[top] = item;
/\ top < MAX;                   top = top + 1;
items[top] = item;              item = 'i';
top = top + 1;                  items[top] = item;
/\!(top == MAX);                top = top + 1;
return 0;                       return 0;
```

Appendix A

```
⇔
/\ 0 < MAX;
/\ 1 < MAX;
/\ 2 < MAX;
/\ 3 > 0;
/\ 2 < MAX;
/\ 3 < MAX;
/\!(4 == MAX);
top = 0;
item = 'd';
items[top] = item;
top = top + 1;
item = 'o';
items[top] = item;
top = top + 1;
item = 'p';
items[top] = item;
top = top + 1;
top = top - 1;
ch = items[top]
item = 'P';
items[top] = item;
top = top + 1;
item = 'i';
items[top] = item;
top = top + 1;
return 0;
```

```
⇔
/\ MAX > 4;
items[0] = 'd';
items[1] = 'o';
items[2] = 'P';
items[3] = 'i';
ch = 'p';
item = 'i';
top = 4;
return 0;
```

Appendix B: Logico-Mathematical Background

In the main text we made extensive use of the concepts and notation developed in propositional calculus, first-order predicate calculus, the principle of mathematical induction, and the regular expression representation of directed graphs. A review is now presented of germane material on these subjects for the benefit of those readers who may not be sufficiently conversant with the subjects.

Propositional Calculus

A *proposition* is a declarative sentence that is either true or false. For example,

> Disney World is located in Florida,
> $x + y = y + x$,
> eleven is divisible by three,
> the number 4 is a prime number,

are propositions. The first two sentences are true, whereas the last two false.

Appendix B

Given propositions, we can form new propositions by combining them with connectives such as "not," "and," "or," etc. Propositional calculus is a method for computing the truth values of propositions that involves connectives.

The connectives of the propositional calculus include

negation: ¬, not
conjunction: ∧, and
disjunction: ∨, or
implication: ⊃, implies, if . . . then . . .
equivalence: ≡, . . . if and only if . . .

The definitions of these connectives are given in the table.

p	q	¬p	p ∧ q	p ∨ q	p ⊃ q	p ≡ q
F	F	T	F	F	T	T
F	T	T	F	T	T	F
T	F	F	F	T	F	F
T	T	F	T	T	T	T

Formally, the propositional calculus is a mathematical system in which $\{T, F\}$ is the underlying set, and the connectives are the operations defined on this set.

A propositional variable is a variable that may assume the value of **T** or F. It denotes a proposition.

A *well-formed formula* (wff) in the language of propositional calculus is a syntactically correct expression. It is composed of connectives, propositional variables (such as p, q, r, s, . . .), constants (**T** and F), and parentheses.

The syntax of a wff can be recursively defined as follows:

1. A propositional variable standing alone is a wff,
2. if α is a wff then $\neg(\alpha)$ is a wff,
3. if α and β are wffs, then $(\alpha) \wedge (\beta)$, $(\alpha) \vee (\beta)$, $(\alpha) \supset (\beta)$, and $(\alpha) \equiv (\beta)$ are wffs,
4. Those and only those obtained by rules 1, 2, and 3 are wffs.

A wff obtained by the preceding definition may contain many parentheses and thus not be suitable for human consumption. The use of parentheses can be reduced by use of the following precedence (listed in descending order):

$$\neg, \wedge, \vee, \supset, \equiv$$

The *truth table* of a wff lists the truth values of the formula for all possible combinations of assignments to the values of variables involved.

In practice, we can often facilitate analysis of a statement by translating it into a well-formed formula first.

Example B.1

Suppose the policy of a pharmaceutical company includes the following statement:

> **Proposition Alpha:** *If the drug passes both animal testing and clinical testing, then the company will market it if and only if it can be produced and sold profitably and the government does not intervene.*

Now let us further suppose that the company is developing a new drug with an enormous market potential, and an ambitious manager has just decided to put the drug on the market immediately, despite the fact that the drug has failed the clinical test. Does this decision to market the drug violate the policy stated as Proposition Alpha?

The policy is not violated if it is not made false. To facilitate determination of its truth value, we translate it into a wff:

$$A_1: \quad a \wedge c \supset (m \equiv p \wedge \neg g),$$

where   a: the drug passes animal testing
           c: the drug passes clinical testing
         m: the company will market the drug
          p: the drug can be produced and sold profitably
          g: the government intervenes

It is obvious that, if the drug failed the clinical test, i.e., if c is false, formula A_1 is true regardless of the assignments of values made to other variables. That is, even though the drug failed to pass the clinical test, the decision to market the drug does not violate the policy represented by A_1.

Note, however, that formula A_1 represents only one possible translation of Proposition Alpha. The same statement can also be taken in such a way that it is translated into the following formula:

A_2 : $a \wedge c \supset m \equiv p \wedge \neg g$.

In this case, "$\equiv$" is the main connective (i.e., the one to be evaluated last, in accordance with the precedence relation defined previously). If c is false, the left-hand side of the "$\equiv$" connective is always true, and the formula becomes false only when the right-hand side of the connective becomes false. Because the truth values of p and g are not given for the question at hand, there is insufficient information to determine the truth value of the formula, and thus the tool should indicate that there is insufficient data to evaluate that proposal to market the drug.

The second translation (A_2) appears to be more plausible. It is hard to imagine that a company would adopt a policy allowing marketing of a drug that did not pass clinical testing.   *End of Example*

Definition B.2

If for every assignment of values to its variables a wff has the value T, the wff is said to be *valid,* or the wff is said to be a *tautology*; if it always has the value F then it is said to be *contradictory* (or a *contradiction*). A wff is said to be *satisfiable* if and only if it is not contradictory. A wff is said to be *contingent* if and only if it is neither valid nor contradictory.

Notation B.3

If A is a tautology, we write $|{-}A$, where "$|{-}$" is "T" written sideways. Note that A is a tautology if and only if $\neg A$ is a contradiction.

It is useful to define certain relationships among propositions so that, if we know the truth value of a proposition, we may be able to say something about the truth values of its relatives. The first relation, a strong one, is logical equivalence.

Definition B.4

Two wffs A and B are said to be *logically equivalent* if and only if they have the same truth table.

Theorem B.5

A and B are logically equivalent if and only if $|-A \equiv B$.

A weaker relation, more frequently encountered in practical applications, is logical consequence.

Definition B.6

B is a *logical consequence* of A (denoted by $A|-B$) if for each assignment of truth value to the variables of A and B such that A has the value T then B also has the value T.

A is called the *antecedent* and B the *consequence* if $A|-B$.

Theorem B.7

$A |- B$ if and only if $|-A \supset B$.

One possible application of this theorem is to establish a rule of inference known as *modus ponens*. This rule says that, if we can show that A and $A \supset B$ are both true, then we can immediately assert that B is also true. The validity of this rule can be established by showing that $|-(A \wedge (A \supset B)) \supset B$.
   Alternatively, the inference rule can be stated as

   if A and $A \supset B$ then B.

Here A corresponds to the premise, $A \supset B$ the argument, and B the conclusion.
   To show that an argument is valid is to show that, whenever the premise is true, the conclusion is also true. In symbolic form, it is to show that $|-A \supset B$. If the argument is valid, we can establish truthfulness of the conclusion simply by showing that the premise is true.

Appendix B

Note that if the premise is a contradiction then there is no way to establish the truthfulness of the conclusion through the use of argument $A \supset B$. Thus, in practical applications, we should check the consistency of the argument. An argument is said to be *consistent* if its premise is satisfiable.

By definition of the implication ($\supset$) connective, $A \supset B$ can be false only if A is true and B is false. Hence a common technique for showing $|- A \supset B$ is to show that, if B is false, it is not possible to (find an assignment of truth values to all prepositional variables involved that will) make A true.

We write $A_1, A_2, \ldots, A_n \mathbin{|-} B$ if the antecedent consists of n propositions such that B is true whenever every component in the antecedent is true.

Theorem B.8

$A_1, A_2, \ldots, A_n \mathbin{|-} B$ if and only if $|- A_1 \wedge A_2 \wedge \ldots \wedge A_n \supset B$.

The relationship $A_1, A_2, \ldots, A_n \mathbin{|-} B$ is useful in that it has the following two properties: (1) when every A_i is true, B is also true; and (2) B is false only if some A_i is false.

This relationship can be used to analyze the validity of a decision. A decision is said to be valid if it does not violate any constraints imposed or contradict any known facts. Constraints may be company policies, government regulations, software requirements, rules of physics, and the like. Let $A_1, A_2, \ldots, A_n$ be the constraints and B be the decision. Then to show that the decision is valid is to show that B is the consequence of $A_1, A_2, \ldots, A_n$, i.e., $|- A_1 \wedge A_2 \wedge \ldots \wedge A_n \supset B$.

A common way to construct the proof of $|- A_1 \wedge A_2 \wedge \ldots \wedge A_n \supset B$ is to show that, if we let B be false, it would be impossible to make all A_i's true at the same time.

It is interesting to see what will happen if additional constraints are imposed on the decision-making process.

Let us suppose that, in addition to the policy expressed as Proposition Alpha, which is repeated below for convenience,

A_1 or A_2: If the drug passes both animal testing and clinical testing, then the company will market it if and only if it can be produced and sold profitably and the government does not intervene

the company further stipulates that

A_3:If the drug cannot be produced and sold profitably, it should not be marketed.

and requires its decision makers to keep in mind that

A_4:If the drug failed the animal test or clinical test and the drug is marketed, the government will definitely intervene.

Also remember that the drug failed the clinical test. This fact is denoted by A_5.

Let us see if the following is a tautology:

$\vdash A_2 \wedge A_3 \wedge A_4 \wedge A_5 \supset B,$

where A_2: $a \wedge c \supset m \equiv p \wedge \neg g$

$\quad\quad A_3$: $\neg p \supset \neg m$

$\quad\quad A_4$: $(\neg a \vee \neg c) \wedge m \supset g$

$\quad\quad A_5$: $\neg c.$

$\quad\quad\rule{4cm}{0.4pt}$

$\quad\quad$ B: $\neg m$

The proof can be constructed as follows.

1. Assume that B is false by assigning F to $\neg m$, i.e., $m \leftarrow$ T.
2. To make A_5 true, $c \leftarrow$ F.
3. To make A_3 true, $p \leftarrow$ T.
4. To make A_4 true, $g \leftarrow$ T.
5. To make A_2 true, we need to do $g \leftarrow$ F. This contradicts what we have done in Step 4.

This shows that it is impossible to make B false and all antecedents (i.e., A_2, A_3, A_4, and A_5) true at the same time, and thus $A_2 \wedge A_3 \wedge A_4 \wedge A_5 \supset B$ is a tautology. That is, the policies represented by A_2, A_3, and A_4, and the fact represented by A_5 dictate that the drug should not be marketed. It is impossible to market the drug without contradicting A_5 or violating at least one of the policies represented by A_2, A_3, and A_4.

Note that the constraints A_2-A_5 are consistent in that it is possible to find an assignment to all propositional variables involved so that all the constraints are true at the same time. See rows 2 and 18 of the following truth table.

It is interesting to observe that $A_1 \land A_3 \land A_4 \land A_5 \supset B$ is not a tautology. The disproof can be constructed in exactly the same way as previously demonstrated except that, in Step 5, we will have to find an assignment to make A_1: $a \land c \supset (m \equiv p \land \neg g)$ true. We will have no problem doing that because A_1 is already made true in Step 2, when we set c to F.

The truth table given at the end of this section may be helpful in clarifying the preceding discussions. Rows corresponding to interesting cases are highlighted. In particular, rows 7 and 23 correspond to the case in which a negative decision can be made without violating any constraints if Proposition Alpha is translated into A_1 instead of A_2.

The truth table is given for

A_1: $a \land c \supset (m \equiv p \land \neg g)$
A_2: $a \land c \supset m \equiv p \land \neg g$
A_3: $\neg p \supset \neg m$
A_4: $(\neg a \lor \neg c) \land m \supset g$
A_5: $\neg c$
B: $\neg m$.

	a	c	m	p	g	A_1	A_2	A_3	A_4	A_5	B
0	F	F	F	F	F	T	F	T	T	T	T
1	F	F	F	F	T	T	F	T	T	T	T
2	F	F	F	T	F	T	T	T	T	T	T
3	F	F	F	T	T	T	F	T	T	T	T
4	F	F	T	F	F	T	F	F	F	T	F
5	F	F	T	F	T	T	F	F	T	T	F
6	F	F	T	T	F	T	T	T	F	T	F
7	F	F	T	T	T	T	F	T	T	T	F
8	F	T	F	F	F	T	F	T	T	F	T
9	F	T	F	F	T	T	F	T	T	F	T
10	F	T	F	T	F	T	T	T	T	F	T
11	F	T	F	T	T	T	F	T	T	F	T

12	F	T	T	F	F	T	F	F	F	F	F
13	F	T	T	F	T	T	F	F	T	F	F
14	F	T	T	T	F	T	T	T	F	F	F
15	F	T	T	T	T	T	F	T	T	F	F
16	**T**	**F**	**F**	**F**	**F**	**T**	**F**	**T**	**T**	**T**	**T**
17	T	F	F	F	T	T	F	T	T	T	T
18	**T**	**F**	**F**	**T**	**F**	**T**	**T**	**T**	**T**	**T**	**T**
19	T	F	F	T	T	T	F	T	T	T	T
20	T	F	T	F	F	T	F	F	F	T	F
21	T	F	T	F	T	T	F	F	T	T	F
22	T	F	T	T	F	T	T	T	F	T	F
23	**T**	**F**	**T**	**T**	**T**	**T**	**F**	**T**	**T**	**T**	**F**
24	T	T	F	F	F	T	T	T	T	F	T
25	T	T	F	F	T	T	T	T	T	F	T
26	T	T	F	T	F	F	F	T	T	F	T
27	T	T	F	T	T	T	T	T	T	F	T
28	T	T	T	F	F	F	F	F	T	F	F
29	T	T	T	F	T	F	F	F	T	F	F
30	T	T	T	T	F	T	T	T	T	F	F
31	T	T	T	T	T	F	F	T	T	F	F

First-Order Predicate Calculus

The power of propositional calculus is quite limited in that it can deal with only propositions, i.e., sentences that are either true or false. In many applications, we have to deal with sentences such as

She is a graduate student.
x > 0.

Without knowing who she is, or what the value of x is, we will not be able to tell if these sentences are true or false. However, once a particular person is assigned to the pronoun "she," or a number is assigned to x, these sentences will become either true or false. These are called *sentential forms*. They cannot be treated in propositional calculus.

First-order predicate calculus can be viewed as an extension of the propositional calculus that includes facilities for handling sentential forms as well as propositions.

The language of first-order predicate calculus includes all symbols for the logical operations and for propositions. In addition, it makes use of the following symbols:

> for individual constants (names of individuals): a, b, c, ... ,
> for individual variables (pronouns): x, y, z, ... ,
> for function letters (to denote functions): f, g, h, ... ,
> for predicate letters (to denote predicates): F, G, H, ... ,
> for quantifiers: universal quantifier ($\forall$x), existential quantifier ($\exists$x).

The syntax of the language can be recursively defined as in the following definition.

Definition B.9

A *term* is defined as follows:

1. Individual constants and individual variables are terms.
2. If f is an n-ary functional letter and $t_1, t_2, \ldots, t_n$ are terms then $f(t_1, t_2, \ldots, t_n)$ is a term.
3. Those and only those obtained by Steps 1 and 2 are terms.

Definition B.10

A string is an *atomic formula* if it is either

1. a propositional variable standing alone, or
2. a string of the form $F(t_1, t_2, \ldots, t_n)$, where F is an n-ary predicate letter and $t_1, t_2, \ldots, t_n$ are terms.

Definition B.11

A *well-formed formula* *(wff)* in the language of first-order predicate calculus is defined as follows:

1. An atomic formula is a wff.
2. If A is a wff and x is an individual variable then ($\forall$x)A and ($\exists$x)A are wffs.
3. If A and B are wffs then $\neg$A, (A) $\wedge$ (B), (A) $\vee$ (B), (A) $\supset$ (B), and (A) $\equiv$ (B) are wffs.
4. Those and only those obtained by Steps 1, 2, or 3 are wffs.

The notation (∀x)P is to be read as "for all x (in the domain)..." and (∃x)P is to be read as "there exists an x (in the domain) such that...".

The *scope* of a quantifier is the subexpression to which the quantifier is applied. The occurrence of an individual variable, say, x, is said to be *bound* if it is either an occurrence (∀x) or (∃x), or within the scope of a quantifier (∀x) or (∃x). Any other occurrence of a variable is a *free* occurrence. For example, in the wff

$$P(x) \land (\exists x)(Q(x) \equiv (\forall y)R(y)),$$

the first occurrence of x is free because it is not within the scope of any quantifier, whereas the second and third occurrences of x and the occurrences of y are all bound. Thus a variable may have both free and bound occurrences within a wff.

A variable may be within the scope of more than one quantifier. In that case, an occurrence of a variable is bound by the innermost quantifier on that variable within whose scope that particular occurrence lies.

Definition B.12

An *interpretation* of a wff consists of a nonempty domain D and an assignment to each n-ary predicate letter of an n-ary predicate on D, to each n-ary function letter of an n-ary function on D, and to each individual constant of a fixed element of D.

Definition B.13

A wff is *satisfiable* in a domain D if there exists an interpretation with domain D and assignments of elements of D to the free occurrences of individual variables in the formula such that the resulting proposition is true.

Definition B.14

A wff is *valid* in a domain D if for every interpretation with domain D and assignment of elements of D to free occurrences of individual variables in the formula the resulting proposition is true.

A wff is satisfiable if it is satisfiable in some domain. A wff is valid if it is valid in all domains.

Appendix B

Example B.15

Consider the wff $(\forall x)P(f(x, a), b)$. A possible interpretation of this wff would be

D:	the set of all integers,
P(u, v):	$u > v$,
f(y, z):	$y + z$,
a:	1,
b:	0.

This interpretation of the wff yields the following statement:

For every integer x, $x + 1 > 0$,

which is obviously false.

Example B.16

Consider the wff $(\forall x)(\exists y)P(f(x, y), a)$. A possible interpretation of this wff would be

D:	the set of all integers,
P(u, v):	u is equal to v,
f(x, y):	$x + y$,
a:	0.

The interpreted formula can be restated as $(\forall x)(\exists y)(x + y = 0)$, and is a true statement.

Observe that the order in which the quantifiers are given is important, and cannot be arbitrarily changed. For instance, if we interchange the quantifiers of the preceding wff, the interpreted statement will change from

For every integer x, there exists another integer y,
such that $x + y = 0$,

which is true, to an entirely different statement

There exists an integer y, such that for every integer x,
$x + y = 0$,

which is obviously false.

Subsequently listed are some theorems in first-order predicate calculus that can be used to govern the movements of quantifiers in a wff.

Theorems B.17

1. $(\exists x)(\exists y)A \equiv (\exists y)(\exists x)A$.
2. $(\forall x)(\forall y)A \equiv (\forall y)(\forall x)A$.
3. $(\forall x)(A \supset B) \equiv ((\exists x)A \supset B)$, where x does not occur free in B.
4. $(\exists x)(A \supset B) \equiv ((\forall x)A \supset B)$, where x does not occur free in B.
5. $(\forall x)(A \supset B) \equiv (A \supset (\forall x)B)$, where x does not occur free in A.
6. $(\exists x)(A \supset B) \equiv (A \supset (\exists x)B)$, where x does not occur free in A.

We can readily verify the correctness of these theorems informally by considering the cases in which the domain is a finite set, say, $D = \{x_1, x_2, \ldots, x_n\}$. Theorem 3, for example, can then be rewritten as

$$(A(x_1) \supset B) \wedge (A(x_2) \supset B) \wedge \ldots \wedge (A(x_n) \supset B)$$

$$\equiv (A(x_1) \vee A(x_2) \vee \ldots \vee A(x_n)) \supset B,$$

and Theorem (4) as

$$(A(x_1) \supset B) \vee (A(x_2) \supset B) \vee \ldots \vee (A(x_n) \supset B)$$

$$\equiv (A(x_1) \wedge A(x_2) \wedge \ldots \wedge A(x_n)) \supset B.$$

Because these can be treated as formulas in propositional calculus, we can readily verify the equivalence relations by using a truth table.

To illustrate the necessity of the qualifier "where x does not occur free in B" for Theorem 3, let us consider the following interpretation, where x occurs free in B(x, y):

D: the set of all positive integers,
A(x, y): x divides y,
B(x, y): $x \leq y$.

With this interpretation, Theorem 3 reads $(\forall x)(\text{"}x \text{ divides } y\text{"} \supset x \leq y) \equiv (\exists x)(x \text{ divides } y) \supset x \leq y$. Although the left-hand side of the "$\equiv$" is true, the truth value of the right-hand side depends on the assignment made to free variable x, and thus the equivalence relation does not hold.

Appendix B

Now if we interpret $B(x, y)$ as $(\exists x)((y \div x)x = y)$, Theorem 3 reads $(\forall x)(\text{"}x \text{ divides } y\text{"} \supset (\exists x)((y \div x)x = y)) \equiv (\exists x)(x \text{ divides } y) \supset (\exists x)((y \div x)x = y)$. The equivalence relation holds because x does not occur free in B.

Note that the equivalence relation also holds if x does not occur in B at all. For example, if we interpret $B(x, y)$ to be "y is not prime" then Theorem 3 reads $(\forall x)(\text{"}x \text{ divides } y\text{"} \supset \text{"}y \text{ is not prime"}) \equiv (\exists x)(x \text{ divides } y) \supset \text{"}y \text{ is not prime."}$

In many cases, the truth value of a wff can be more readily evaluated if we transform the wff into the canonical form subsequently described.

Definition B.18

A wff is said to be in the *prenex normal form* if it is of the form

$$(Q_1 x_1)(Q_2 x_2) \ldots (Q_n x_n) M,$$

where each $(Q_i x_i)$ is either $(\forall x_i)$ or $(\exists x_i)$ and M is a formula containing no quantifiers. $(Q_1 x_1)(Q_2 x_2) \ldots (Q_n x_n)$ is called the *prefix* and M the *matrix* of the formula.

The following rules (logically equivalent relations) can be utilized to transform a given wff into its prenex normal form:

1a. $\neg((\exists x)A(x)) \equiv (\forall x)(\neg A(x))$.
1b. $\neg((\forall x)A(x)) \equiv (\exists x)(\neg A(x))$.
2a. $(Qx)A(x) \vee B \equiv (Qx)(A(x) \vee B)$, where x does not occur free in B.
2b. $(Qx)A(x) \wedge B \equiv (Qx)(A(x) \wedge B)$, where x does not occur free in B.
3a. $(\exists x)A(x) \vee (\exists x)C(x) \equiv (\exists x)(A(x) \vee C(x))$.
3b. $(\forall x)A(x) \wedge (\forall x)C(x) \equiv (\forall x)(A(x) \wedge C(x))$.
4a. $(Q_1 x)A(x) \vee (Q_2 x)C(x) \equiv (Q_1 x)(Q_2 y)(A(x) \vee C(y))$.
4b. $(Q_3 x)A(x) \wedge (Q_4 x)C(x) \equiv (Q_3 x)(Q_4 y)(A(x) \wedge C(y))$.

Here, in 4a and 4b, y is a variable that does not occur in $A(x)$. Q, Q_1, Q_2, Q_3, and Q_4 are either $\exists$ or $\forall$.

To make the preceding rules applicable, it may be necessary to rename variables and rewrite the formula into an equivalent one with $\neg$, $\wedge$, and $\vee$ connectives only.

Example B.19

Consider the wff $(\forall x)P(x) \wedge (\exists x)Q(x) \vee \neg(\exists x)R(x)$, which can be rewritten into the prenex normal form as follows.

$(\forall x)P(x) \wedge (\exists x)Q(x) \vee \neg(\exists x)R(x)$
$(\forall x)P(x) \wedge (\exists x)Q(x) \vee (\forall x)(\neg R(x))$ by rule 1a
$(\forall x)(\exists y)(P(x) \wedge Q(y)) \vee (\forall x)(\neg R(x))$ by rule 4b
$(\forall x)(\exists y)(\forall z)(P(x) \wedge Q(y) \vee \neg R(z))$ by rule 4a

This sequence of transformation is valid provided that x does not occur free in Q and R, y does not occur free in P and R, and z does not occur free in P and Q. In applying the transformation rules, always select a new variable name such that no free variable becomes bound in the process.

To illustrate, let us consider the following logical expression:

$$b - a > e \wedge b + 2a \geq 6 \wedge 2(b - a)/3 \leq e. \tag{A}$$

In program testing, the preceding expression may represent the condition under which a specific program path will be traversed, and the problem is to find an assignment of values to the input variables a, b, and e such that the condition is satisfied.

An inequality solver can be used to find possible solutions to (A). Alternatively, if we find it easier to work with equalities, we can restate formula (A) in terms of equality by observing that

$a > b \equiv (\exists d)_{d>0}(a = b + d),$
$a \geq b \equiv (\exists d)_{d \geq 0}(a = b + d),$
$a < b \equiv (\exists d)_{d>0}(a = b - d),$
$a \leq b \equiv (\exists d)_{d \geq 0}(a = b - d).$

Formula (A) thus becomes

$$(\exists x)_{D_1}(x = b - a - e) \wedge (\exists x)_{D_2}(x = b + 2a - 6)$$
$$\wedge (\exists x)_{D_2}(x = e - 2(b - a)/3),$$

where D_1 is the set of all real numbers greater than 0 and D_2 is the set of all real numbers greater than or equal to 0.

Appendix B

We can make the task more manageable by rewriting it into its prenex normal form:

$$(\exists x)_{D_1}(\exists y)_{D_2}(\exists z)_{D_2}(x = b - a - e \land y = b + 2a - 6$$
$$\land z = e - 2(b - a)/3). \tag{B}$$

The preceding three equations are indeterminate because there are more than three variables involved. Therefore we cannot directly obtain the desired assignment by solving the equations. However, we can combine these three equations to form a new equation in such a way that the number of variables involved in the new equation will be minimal. We can accomplish this by using the same techniques we use in solving simultaneous equations. In the present example, we can combine the three equations to yield

$$(\exists x)_{D_1}(\exists y)_{D_2}(\exists z)_{D_2}(3x - y + 3z = 6 - 3a). \tag{C}$$

As indicated in the preceding expression, the requirements on the assignments to x, y, and z are that $x > 0$, $y \geq 0$, and $z \geq 0$. So let us begin by making the following assignments:

$$x \leftarrow 0.1, \qquad y \leftarrow 0, \qquad z \leftarrow 0.$$

Then (C) can be satisfied by letting

$$a \leftarrow 1.9.$$

To satisfy the second component in (B) we must have $0 = b + 2 \times 1.9 - 6 = b - 2.2$, i.e., we have to make the assignment

$$b \leftarrow 2.2.$$

Finally, the first and the third components of (B) can be satisfied by letting

$$e \leftarrow 0.2.$$

In summary, logical expression (A) can be satisfied by the following assignment:

$$a \leftarrow 1.9, \qquad b \leftarrow 2.2, \qquad e \leftarrow 0.2.$$

Principle of Mathematical Induction

The set of all (nonnegative) integers have many interesting properties, and chief among them are that (1) the numbers can be constructed (or generated) from 0 uniquely, and (2) if a property that holds for one number also holds for the next number in the generation, then that property holds for all integers.

The second property noted is the gist of the principle of mathematical induction, which has so many applications in computer programming that it requires some discussion.

Definition B.20

Principle of mathematical induction: If 0 has a property P, and if any integer n is P, then n + 1 is also P, and then every integer is P. The principle is used in proving statements about integers or, derivatively, in proving statements about sets of objects of any kind that can be correlated with integers.

The procedure is to prove that

   a. 0 is P (induction basis),
        to assume that
   b. n is P (induction hypothesis),
        to prove that
   c. n+1 is P (induction step)
        using Steps a and b; and then to conclude that
   d. n is P for all n.

For example, suppose we wish to prove that

$$\sum_{i=0}^{n} i = \frac{n(n+1)}{2}.$$

To begin, we must state the property that we want to prove. This statement is called the induction proposition. In this case P is directly given by

$$n \text{ is } P \Leftrightarrow \sum_{i=0}^{n} i = \frac{n(n+1)}{2}.$$

Appendix B

a. For the basis of the induction we have, for $n = 0$, $0 = \frac{0(0+1)}{2}$, which is true.

b. The induction hypothesis is that k is P for some arbitrarily choice of k:

$$\sum_{i=0}^{k} i = 0 + 1 + 2 + \cdots + k = \frac{k(k+1)}{2}.$$

c. For the induction step, proving $k + 1$ is P, we have

$$\sum_{i=0}^{k+1} i = \sum_{i=0}^{k} i + (k+1) = \frac{k(k+1)}{2} + (k+1)$$

$$\text{(using the induction hypothesis)}$$

$$= \frac{kk + k + 2k + 2}{2}$$

$$= \frac{(k+1)((k+1)+1)}{2}.$$

d. Hence $k + 1$ has the property P.

The principle of induction is also valid if, at Step b, the induction hypothesis, we assume that every $k \leq n$ is P. Moreover, we may choose any integer as a basis and then prove that some property of interest holds for the set of integers greater than or equal to the basis.

A closely related concept, which is commonly used in computer programming, is the inductive definition of a set or property having the standard form.

Definition B.21

Inductive definition of a set or property P: given a finite set A:

a. the elements of A are P (basis clause),
b. the elements of B, all of which are constructed from A, are P (inductive clause),
c. the elements constructed as in a and b are the only elements of P (extremal clause).

We have already seen many examples of inductive definitions in the preceding section, in which all well-formed formulas are defined inductively.

Directed Graphs and Path Descriptions

As explained in Chapter 5, the path structures in a directed graph can be conveniently described by use of regular expressions. For example, the set of paths between nodes 1 and 4 in the following graph shown below can be described by using a regular expression, such as $a(e+bc*d)$ or $ae+abd+abc*d$.

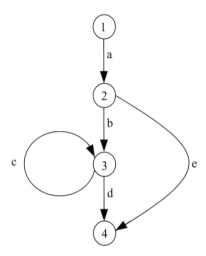

The question now is this: Given a directed graph, how do we go about finding a regular expression that describes the path structure between a pair of nodes in the graph? Subsequently presented is a method that can be used to answer this question systematically (Lunts, 1965). It is easy to understand, and it is relatively easy to implement on a computer.

Let G be a directed graph in which each edge is labeled by an element of set E of symbols. If there are n nodes in G, then G can be represented by an $n \times n$ matrix as follows. First, the nodes in G are to be ordered in some way. Then we form an $n \times n$ matrix $[G] = [g_{ij}]$, where g_{ij} (the element on the ith row and jth column) is a regular expression denoting the set of all paths of length 1 (i.e., the paths formed by a single edge) leading from the ith node to the jth node.

Appendix B

For example, the graph in the preceding figure can be represented by the following matrix:

$$\begin{bmatrix} \emptyset & a & \emptyset & \emptyset \\ \emptyset & \emptyset & b & e \\ \emptyset & \emptyset & c & d \\ \emptyset & \emptyset & \emptyset & \emptyset \end{bmatrix},$$

where $\emptyset$ is a special symbol representing the empty set.

The operation of concatenation, disjunction $(+)$, and star operation $(*)$ are now to be extended over the matrices with regular expressions as elements. Let $[X]$, $[Y]$, $[Z]$, and $[W]$ be $n \times n$ matrices. We define

$$[X] + [Y] = [Z] = [z_{ij}],$$

where $z_{ij} = x_{ij} + y_{ij}$,

$$[X][Y] = [W] = [w_{ij}],$$

where $w_{ij} = +_{k=1}^{n} x_{ik} y_{kj}$, and

$$[X]^* = [X]^0 + [X]^1 + [X]^2 + [X]^3 + \dots,$$

where $[X]_0$ is defined to be an $n \times n$ matrix in which every element on the main diagonal is λ and all other elements are identically $\emptyset$. If we consider concatenation as multiplication and disjunction as addition, then the first two matrix operations just defined are similar to matrix addition and matrix multiplication, respectively, defined in the theory of matrices.

Now given $[G] = [g_{ij}]$, the matrix representation of a graph G having n nodes, we may construct an $(n-1) \times (n-1)$ matrix B by simultaneously eliminating the kth row and the kth column of $[G]$ (for some $1 \leq k \leq n$)

as follows:

$$[G] = \begin{bmatrix} g_{11} & \cdots & g_{1k} & \cdots & g_{1n} \\ \cdots & & & & \cdots \\ g_{k1} & \cdots & g_{kk} & \cdots & g_{kn} \\ \cdots & & & & \cdots \\ g_{n1} & \cdots & g_{nk} & \cdots & g_{nn} \end{bmatrix},$$

$$[B] = \begin{bmatrix} g_{11} & \cdots & g_{1(k-1)} & g_{1(k+1)} & \cdots & g_{1n} \\ \cdots & & & & & \cdots \\ g_{(k-1)1} & \cdots & g_{(k-1)(k-1)} & g_{(k-1)(k+1)} & \cdots & g_{(k-1)n} \\ g_{(k+1)1} & \cdots & g_{(k+1)(k-1)} & g_{(k+1)(k+1)} & \cdots & g_{(k+1)n} \\ \cdots & & & & & \cdots \\ g_{n1} & \cdots & g_{n(k-1)} & g_{n(k+1)} & & g_{nn} \end{bmatrix}$$

$$+ \begin{bmatrix} g_{1k} \\ \cdots \\ g_{(k-1)k} \\ g_{(k+1)k} \\ \cdots \\ g_{nk} \end{bmatrix} \begin{bmatrix} g_{kk} \end{bmatrix}^* \begin{bmatrix} g_{k1} & \cdots & g_{k(k-1)} & g_{k(k+1)} & \cdots & g_{kn} \end{bmatrix}.$$

It should be easy to see that eliminating a row and the corresponding column in [G] in this way does not alter the path information between any pair of the remaining nodes. On the right-hand side of the preceding equation, the first term represents all the paths that do not go through the node to be eliminated and the second term represents all the paths that do. In other words, matrix [B] represents the graph we obtain by eliminating the kth node in the original graph without removing the associated edges.

Thus to find the paths leading from the ith node to the jth node in G, we simply use the method just described to successively eliminate (in any order) all nodes other than the ith and the jth nodes. We are then left with a 2×2 matrix (assuming i < j):

$$[B'] = \begin{bmatrix} b_{ii} & b_{ij} \\ b_{ji} & b_{jj} \end{bmatrix}.$$

Then p_{ij}, the regular expression denoting the paths leading from the ith node to the jth node can be constructed from the elements in [B′] as follows:

$$p - ij = (b_{ii} + b_{ij}b_{jj}^*b_{ji})^* b_{ij}(b_{jj} + b_{ji}b_{ii}^*b_{ij})^*.$$

If $b_{ii} = b_{ji} = b_{jj} = \emptyset$, which is almost always the case in many applications, then we have

$$p_{ij} = b_{ij},$$

because $\emptyset^* = \lambda$ and $\lambda a = a\lambda = a$ for any regular expression a.

To illustrate, let us suppose that we wish to find the set of all paths leading from node 1 to node 4 in the graph given in the preceding figure. The matrix representation of the graph is repeated for convenience:

$$\begin{bmatrix} \emptyset & a & \emptyset & \emptyset \\ \emptyset & \emptyset & b & e \\ \emptyset & \emptyset & c & d \\ \emptyset & \emptyset & \emptyset & \emptyset \end{bmatrix}.$$

According to the method just described, we can eliminate, for example, column 2 and row 2 (i.e., node 2) first to yield the following 3×3 matrix:

$$\begin{bmatrix} \emptyset & \emptyset & \emptyset \\ \emptyset & c & d \\ \emptyset & \emptyset & \emptyset \end{bmatrix} + \begin{bmatrix} a \\ \emptyset \\ \emptyset \end{bmatrix} [\emptyset]^* \begin{bmatrix} \emptyset & b & e \end{bmatrix}$$

$$= \begin{bmatrix} \emptyset & \emptyset & \emptyset \\ \emptyset & c & d \\ \emptyset & \emptyset & \emptyset \end{bmatrix} + \begin{bmatrix} \emptyset & ab & ae \\ \emptyset & \emptyset & \emptyset \\ \emptyset & \emptyset & \emptyset \end{bmatrix}$$

$$= \begin{bmatrix} \emptyset & ab & ae \\ \emptyset & c & d \\ \emptyset & \emptyset & \emptyset \end{bmatrix}.$$

Now column 2 and row 2 correspond to the node labeled by integer 3. It can be similarly eliminated to yield the following 2×2 matrix:

$$\begin{bmatrix} \emptyset & ae \\ \emptyset & \emptyset \end{bmatrix} + \begin{bmatrix} ab \\ \emptyset \end{bmatrix} [c]^* [\emptyset \quad d]$$

$$= \begin{bmatrix} \emptyset & ae \\ \emptyset & \emptyset \end{bmatrix} + \begin{bmatrix} \emptyset & abc^*d \\ \emptyset & \emptyset \end{bmatrix}$$

$$= \begin{bmatrix} \emptyset & ae + abc^*d \\ \emptyset & \emptyset \end{bmatrix}.$$

Hence set of paths leading from node 1 to node 4 is described by ae+abc*d.

The reader may wonder what will happen if we eliminate the nodes in a different order. In general, different regular expressions will result if the nodes are eliminated in different orders, but the resulting regular expressions will be equivalent in the sense that they all denote the same set. Therefore we may say that the order in which the nodes are eliminated is immaterial insofar as the membership of the path set is concerned. But in some applications, the resulting regular expression represents a program composed of a set of path subprograms. The complexity of the regular expression reflects the complexity of the program. In such applications, therefore, it may be desirable to eliminate the nodes in the order that will yield a regular expression of the least (syntactic) complexity. An algorithm for determining such an order, however, remains unknown.

Proving Programs Correct

Finally, without going into detail, it is explained how the correctness proof of a program can be constructed.

A common task in proving the correctness of a program is to show that, for a given program S, if a certain *precondition* Q is true before the execution of S then a certain *postcondition* R is true after the execution, provided that S terminates. This logical proposition is commonly denoted by Q{S}R for short [a notation that is due to Hoare (1969)]. If we succeeded in showing that Q{S}R is a theorem (i.e., always true), then to show that S is *partially*[1] correct, with respect to some input predicate I and output predicate $\oslash$, is to show that I $\supset$ Q and R $\supset \oslash$.

---

[1] The correctness proven is partial in that the termination property is not included.

Appendix B

Alternatively the correctness proof of a program, say S, with respect to postcondition R, can also be constructed by use of wp(S, R), a predicate transformation function. As defined by Dijkstra (1976), wp(S, R) denotes the weakest precondition of program S with postcondition R. To be more explicit, it is the weakest condition for the initial state of S such that activation of S will certainly result in a proper termination of execution of S, leaving it in a final state satisfying R. Program S is *totally* correct with respect input predicate I and output predicate $\oslash$ if we can find some predicates R such that I $\supset$ wp(S, R) and R $\supset$ $\oslash$. In that case, we write I[S]$\oslash$.

The present analysis method can also be used to construct a correctness proof. It is obvious from the discussion in Chapter 6 that program S is partially correct with respect to input predicate I and output predicate $\oslash$ if we can show that $/\backslash$I;S;$/\backslash\oslash \Leftrightarrow /\backslash$I;S, i.e., if we can show that $/\backslash\oslash$ is a tautological constraint in $/\backslash$I;S;$/\backslash\oslash$.

References

Aho, A. V., Sethi, R., and Ullman, J. D., *Compilers: Principles, Techniques, and Tools*, Addison-Wesley, Reading, MA, 1986.

Aho, A. V. and Ullman, J. D., *The Theory of Parsing, Translation, and Compiling, Vol. II: Compiling*, Prentice-Hall, Englewood Cliffs, NJ, 1973.

Aiken, A., "Introduction to set constraint-based program analysis," *Science of Computer Programming* **35**, (2–3), 79–111, 1999.

Ammons, G. and Larus, J. R., "Improving Data-Flow Analysis with Path Profiles," *Proceedings of the ACM SIGPLAN 1998 Conference on Programming Language Design and Implementation*, Montreal, Quebec, 1998, 72–84.

Amtoft, T., Nielson, F., and Nielson, H. R., *Type and Effect Systems: Behaviours for Concurrency*, World Scientific, Singapore, 1999.

Anderson, R. B., *Proving Programs Correct*, John Wiley & Sons, New York, NY, 1979.

Charniak, E. and McDermott, D., *Introduction to Artificial Intelligence*, Addison-Wesley, Reading, MA, 1985, p. 147.

Cousot, P. and Cousot, R., "Abstract interpretation: A unified lattice model for static analysis of programs by construction or approximation of fixpoints," in the *Proceeding of the ACM Symposium on Principles of Programming Languages*, Association for Computing Machinery, New York, NY, 1977, pp. 238–52.

Dijkstra, E. W., "Guarded commands, nondeterminancy and formal derivation of programs," *Communications of the ACM* **18**, 453–7, 1975.

References

Dijkstra, E. W., *A Discipline of Programming*, Prentice-Hall, Englewood Cliffs, NJ, 1976.

Flanagan, C. and Qadeer, S., "A type and effect system for atomicity," *ACM SIGPLAN Notices* **38**, 338–49, 2003.

Fosdick, L. D. and Osterweil, L. J., "Data flow analysis in software reliability," *ACM Computing Surveys* **8**, 305–30, 1976.

Gehani, N., *ADA: An Advanced Introduction*, Prentice-Hall, Englewood Cliffs, NJ, 1983.

Howden, W. E. and Eichhorst, P., "Proving properties of Programs from program traces," CS Report #18, University of California at San Diego, 1977.

Huang, J. C., "A new verification rule and its applications," *IEEE Transactions on Software Engineering* **SE6**, 480–4, 1980a.

Huang, J. C., "Instrumenting programs for symbolic-trace generation," *Computer* **13**, 17–23, 1980b.

Huang, J. C., "State constraints and pathwise decomposition of programs," *IEEE Transactions on Software Engineering* **16**, 880–96, 1990.

Huang, J. C. and Leng, T., "Generalized loop-unrolling: A method for program speedup" in *Proceedings of the 1999 IEEE Workshop on Application-Specific Software Engineering and Technology,* IEEE, 1999, pp. 244–8.

Johnsonbaugh, R. and Kalin, M., *Application Programming in C++*, Prentice-Hall, Englewood Cliff, NJ, 1999.

Jones, N. D. and Nielson, F., "Abstract interpretation: A semantics-based tool for program analysis," in *Handbook of Logic in Computer Science, Vol. 4: Semantic Modeling*, Oxford University Press, New York, NY, 1995.

Jalote, P., Vangala, V., Singh, T., and Jain, P., "Program partitioning: A framework for combining static and dynamic analysis," in *Proceedings of the 2006 International Workshop on Dynamic Systems Analysis*, ACM Press, 2006, pp. 11–16.

Khurshid, S., Păsăreanu, C. S., and Visser, W., "Generalized symbolic execution for model checking and testing," In H. Garavel and J. Hatcliff, editors, *Tools and Algorithms for the Construction and Analysis of Systems*, 9th International Conference, TACAS 2003, Held as Part of the Joint European Conferences on Theory and Practice of Software, ETAPS 2003, Warsaw, Poland, 2003, Proceedings, volume 2619 of Lecture Notes in Computer Science, Springer, 2003.

King, J. C., "A new approach to program testing," in *Proceeding of the 1975 International Conference on Reliable Software*, ACM Press, 1975.

King, J. C., "Symbolic Execution and Program Testing," *Communications of te ACM* **19**, 385–94, 1976.

Leler, W., *Constraint programming languages: Their specification and generation*, Addison-Wesley, Reading, MA, 1988.

Leng, T., *Program Speedup Through Generalized Loop Unrolling: Practical Aspects*, Ph.D. dissertation, Department of Computer Science, University of Houston, Houston, TX, 2001.

References

Lunts, A. G., "A method of analysis of finite automata," *Soviet Physics – Doklady* **10**, 102–3, 1965.

Manna, Z., *Mathematical Theory of Computation*, McGraw-Hill, New York, NY, 1974.

McCabe, T. J., "A complexity measure," *IEEE Transactions on Software Engineering* **SE2**, 308–20, 1976.

Nielson, F., Nielson, H. R., and Hankin, C., *Principles of Program Analysis*, 2nd ed., Springer-Verlag, New York, NY, 2005.

Prata, S., *C++ Primer Plus*, 5th ed., Sams Publishing, Indianapolis, 2005.

Stucki, L. G., "Automatic generation of self-metric software," in *Proceedings of the IEEE Symposium on Computer Software Reliability*, IEEE, New York, NY, 1973, pp. 94–100.

Weiser, M., "Program Slicing," *IEEE Transactions on Software Engineering*, **SE-10**, 1984, 352–7.

WIKIPEDIA: The Internet free encyclopedia, available at http://en.wikipedia.org.

Yeh, R. T., "Verification of programs by predicate transformation," in *Current Trends in Programming Methodology, Vol. II: Program Validation*, Prentice-Hall, Englewood Cliffs, NJ, 1977, pp. 228–47.

Index

Index